NATIVE RELIGIONS
OF
NORTH AMERICA

NATIVE RELIGIONS
OF
NORTH AMERICA

The Power of Visions
and Fertility

ÅKE HULTKRANTZ

WAVELAND
PRESS, INC.
Prospect Heights, Illinois

For information about this book, write or call:
Waveland Press, Inc.
P.O. Box 400
Prospect Heights, Illinois 60070
847/634-0081

For Geraldine

Contents

Preface

North American aboriginal religions represent a vast subject, and no introductory book can do justice to their immense richness and variety. This work should be considered a brief introduction to the study of these religions. It attempts to provide an orientation to the American Indian religious world and at the same time an insight into the structure and functioning of living tribal religions.

To this end the book has been divided into two main parts. The first part, designed to cover the most essential features and the basic scope of Native American religions, presents a general overview of the most important phenomena and historical developments (where these may be traced). The second part sketches two separate religions that illustrate the two main branches of religious expression among the Native peoples: the religions of the hunters and the religions of the agriculturists. Like most other religions outside the range of Eurasiatic more complex religions, North American indigenous religions are, in their organizational structure and choice of religious imagery, dependent on the nature around them and on their ecological use of this nature. This is why the division into "hunting religion" and "agricultural religion" is so important.

There are of course many variations in these two main types of religions in North America, and the two I have selected certainly do not exhaust the possibilities in matters of religious expression and religious organization. Still, they are representative of the tendencies in the two structural religious patterns. The agricultural Zuni of New Mexico were selected because of their tendency toward organization, a tendency that has made their religion the most complex in aboriginal North America. The Wind River Shoshoni, hunting Indians on the western high plains, are the Indians among whom I conducted field work during a number of years (particularly 1948–1958). Their religion is presented in some detail here for the first time. Both religions manifest the historical depth of their traditions, and the faithfulness of the people, particularly the Zuni, to these traditions is evident in these pages. At the same time there is a continuous innovative process going on, particularly among the Shoshoni, that recreates religion in new patterns. During the last decades pan-Indianism and secularization have changed many old religious forms.

It is my hope that this little volume will illuminate both the traditional religions and the major changes they have undergone. I also trust that it will open the richness and beauty of American Indian religion to a larger public.

For linguistic help and preparation of maps I am indebted to my dear wife, Geraldine. As a small token of my gratitude I dedicate the book to her. Any my thoughts go also to my Shoshoni friends, many now deceased, who with such dedication of spirit initiated me into Shoshoni religion.

Å.H.

Chronology of Native American Culture and Religion

(with particular references to Shoshoni and Zuni history)

Chronology	Major Cultural and Religious Features

FIRST INHABITANTS

60,000–30,000 years ago	Arrival of groups of peoples from northeast Asia, carriers of a circumpolar and circumboreal hunting culture. Religion: animal ceremonialism, masters of the animals, shamanism.
4000 B.C.E.–birth of Christ	Last immigrants of prehistoric times: the Athapascan Indians. Religion: hunting religion, girls' puberty rites.

PREHISTORIC DEVELOPMENTS

8000–5000 B.C.E.	Immigrants reach Tierra del Fuego. In North America increase in population density and

3

differentiation into two great cultural traditions: the Archaic hunting tradition east of the Rockies and the "Desert" (or "Desert Archaic" or "Western Archaic") culture in the greater Southwest (including California, the Plateau, and northwestern Mexico). The latter was adapted to the harvesting of acorns, piñon nuts, grass seeds, roots, and berries. Religion: rituals around the gathering of plant foods, an attenuated shamanism. (This is partly the basis of Shoshoni religion.)

5000 B.C.E.

Introduction of agriculture in Central America, followed by settlement in villages, the construction of ritual centers and burial mounds, and social and ceremonial differentiation. Religion: plant spirits, ceremonial calendar, incipient cult of the dead, sacred rulers.

1500 B.C.E.–1000 C.E.

Formative period of Mexican civilizations. Growth of city culture, with temples and plazas, sacred kings and powerful gods. These cultures have had an impact on those of North America.

1000 B.C.E.	Eastern Woodlands cultures, influenced from Mexico, with houses on mounds formed like birds, and burials in mounds. Presence of Mother Earth statuettes.
300 B.C.E.–700 C.E.	Hopewell culture in the Ohio area and its surroundings, characterized by burial mounds, ceremonial centers and cosmological symbolism, but very little agriculture.
1–500 C.E.	Beginning of maize farming settlements in the Southwest and ceremonial constructions inspired from Mexico. Original habitations in the eastern part of the area were pit houses, which later became the Pueblo ceremonial chambers.
700–800	Possible origin of the Zuni pueblo in the Southwestern Basketmaker period. Mississippian culture period, stimulated from Mexico, with maize agriculture, platform mounds and sacred kings, and rich ceremonial symbolism. Its fertility religion and elaborate ceremonies (called the "Southern cult," or "Southeastern Ceremonial complex") radiated out over the Eastern Woodlands cultures.
1000–1200	Building of Zuni pueblo houses.

1000–1400	Mississippian culture invades the eastern plains, or prairies, introducing horticulture and cosmological symbolism and ceremonialism. Part of this complex sifted into the tribes of the western high plains, which were not semisedentary, however, but nomadic.
1100–1200	Founding of the Hopi pueblo of Oraibi.

HISTORICAL TIMES

1540–1541	Arrival in Zuni ("Cibola") of Spanish expedition under Francisco Vasquez Coronado, who then continued to the southern Plains.
1598	Beginning of Franciscan missionary activities in Zuni.
1629	First mission established in Zuni.
1680–1692	The Pueblo rebellion against the Spaniards. Thereafter concentration of the Zuni population to one pueblo and the desertion of five others. Rearrangement of Zuni ritual organization.
1699	The main church in Zuni is erected.
1700–1800	Invasion of northern and eastern tribes into the Plains area as a consequence of white population pressure. The Sun Dance complex is

	diffused to most Plains tribes from intruding groups.
1775–1825	Restructuring of Shoshoni religion in Wyoming: general vision quest, Sun Dance, high-god concept activated.
1868	Creation of the Wind River Reservation for Plains Shoshoni and Sheepeaters.
1877	Creation of Zuni Reservation.
1883	Episcopal mission opened at Wind River.
1890	Introduction of Christian symbolism into the Sun Dance at Wind River. Ghost Dance.
1919	Introduction of the peyote religion on the Wind River Reservation.

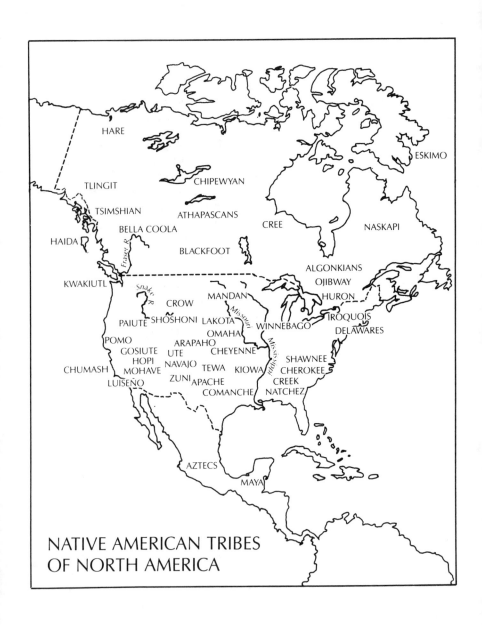

HARE

ESKIMO

TLINGIT

CHIPEWYAN

TSIMSHIAN

ATHAPASCANS

BELLA COOLA

Fraser R.

CREE

NASKAPI

HAIDA

BLACKFOOT

KWAKIUTL

Snake R.

CROW

MANDAN

ALGONKIANS

OJIBWAY

HURON

PAIUTE SHOSHONI

Missouri

LAKOTA

WINNEBAGO

IROQUOIS

DELAWARES

POMO

OMAHA

ARAPAHO

CHEYENNE

GOSIUTE UTE

HOPI

Mississippi

SHAWNEE

CHUMASH MOHAVE NAVAJO TEWA KIOWA CHEROKEE

LUISEÑO ZUNI APACHE CREEK

COMANCHE NATCHEZ

AZTECS

MAYA

NATIVE AMERICAN TRIBES
OF NORTH AMERICA

CHAPTER I

Introduction to Native American Religions

The Diversity and Richness of American Indian Religions

The religious life of Native Americans is a rich panorama featuring many diverse beliefs, ceremonies, and ways of life, but little of this rich tradition is reflected in the popular notions about these peoples. Probably the most familiar image of the "American Indian" is the Plains Indian, whose life centered around the hunt; in it we see Plains Indians of recent centuries riding horses to hunt buffalo (bison). However, this popular image presents an incomplete picture of American Indians—it overlooks the farming heritage of Native Americans and does not even scratch the surface of their ancient hunting culture and related religious beliefs and practices. These Native Americans of the Plains shared not only a hunting culture, but also a common religious heritage, especially a midsummer **Sun Dance*** that emphasized the bravery, courage, and individual initiative so highly prized by these hunting people. Although the horse is a rather recent newcomer to the Americas (having been introduced by the Spaniards in the sixteenth century), a hunting life and the religious rituals associated with hunting were important for all Native American cultures, even the sophisticated Maya, Aztecs, and Incas in Central and South America.

These hunting rituals can tell us something about the religious

---

*Terms defined in the Glossary are printed boldface where they first appear in text.

9

life not only of Native Americans, but also of the so-called world religions. In fact, many of the spiritual ideas and ritual expressions of contemporary religions—even Christianity—have their origins in hunting religions of the same type as those found in North and South America. One reason those of us who are not Native Americans study their religious beliefs and customs is to recover a religious heritage that we all, as descendants of hunters in ages past, share.

Another more important reason for studying American Indian religions is their intrinsic interest. Just as Native American cultures exhibit a colorful series of tribal or "national" life-styles (not limited to the pattern of horse-riding hunters on the Plains), so too the religions of these cultures provide a rich and varied tapestry of approaches to the supernatural. Indigenous American religions are as dramatic and exciting as the art forms they express themselves in. These traditions possess a treasure trove of myths and tales of all varieties, some humorous and even obscene, others beautiful and highly spiritual. These traditions also contain beliefs and ideas about the world that achieve high levels of sophistication, as in the notions about the beginning of the world, the concepts of a lofty Supreme Being, and the elaboration of cosmic harmony. In ritual, too, the Native American traditions present a rich and varied heritage of dramatic beauty and spiritual force, primarily expressed in dancing and repetitive movements, prayers, and songs.

Some people, and even some scholars, have viewed Native American religions as examples of what has been called "primitive religion." If by "primitive" is meant crude cultural manifestations devoid of deeper feelings and subtle thoughts, American Indian religions are far from primitive. Some scholars of religion who specialize in the study of world religions but are not familiar with the rich symbolism and profound speculative thought in Native American religions neglected them in their consideration of comparative religion. This is an unfortunate mistake, based on a lack of concrete knowledge of American Indians and a misconception about their "primitive" character. It is unfortunate because it overlooks a treasury of myths and tales, speculative thought, and ritual activity. Indeed, questions about the creation of the world, the origin of human life, the nature of the divine or supernatural, and the afterlife—all topics discussed in the "advanced" world religions—have also been posed by the indigenous religions of North and South America.

Such questions are found among all peoples and occur in all cultures, even though the "answers" to these questions are distinctively different in each tradition. By studying the Native American answers we will learn not only about their traditions but become more sensitive to the answers of our own traditions.

It is difficult to generalize about Native American cultures and religions because in the Americas there are a multitude of tribes and other social units. The diversity of these traditions cannot be reduced to a single tradition, for there is no simple entity such as "*the* Native American religion." A number of tribes may be grouped together because they participate in a similar cultural life, such as the buffalo hunting tribes on the Plains or the fishing and manioc cultivators in the Amazonian lowlands. These tribes that share a similar cultural life also tend to share a similar religious life. Nevertheless, each tribe has its own practices and customs, and we must remember that there are as many Native American religions as there are tribes.

No single book can present a satisfactory survey of all these religions. The purpose of this brief book is to first provide some general information on all Native American religions, and then focus more closely on two examples of Native American religions in North America. This chapter takes up the thorny question of the origin and development of Native American religions, considering the manner in which these traditions were formed and how this helps us understand the rather flexible character of these traditions. The second chapter discusses some general features of all Native American religions. Chapters III and IV provide case studies of two contrasting examples of Native American traditions, the Wind River Shoshoni of the Utah and Wyoming area and the Zuni of the American Southwest. Each tradition will be presented and discussed through its historical development, its structure as a religious tradition, and examples of its religious dynamics.

Ethnic and Religious Origins

Native Americans did not keep written records of their history, and the written records by Europeans cover only the time since the arrival of Columbus in 1492. Of course Native Americans preserve an oral tradition of their beliefs and customs, but this does not include a close sequence of historical events. And the history recorded by whites has been distorted and fragmentary. For all these reasons it is not possible to reconstruct the history of Zuni or Shoshoni culture over a long span of time such as can be done, for example, with ancient Greece and Rome. The earliest documents on the Zuni date from 1540, and the Zuni themselves have been hesitant about providing information to outsiders. For the Shoshoni detailed information was lacking until the beginning of the nineteenth century.

A similar lack of historical information holds for the rest of native North America. In spite of the collection and publication of much ethnographic information during the past century, we still do not know the full story of the historical development of American Indian religions. However, the general knowledge we have of the historical and cultural background of North American Indian religions can be summarized briefly as a means of throwing light on the contrast between Shoshoni and Zuni.

The origins of Native Americans are found in the migration of groups of northeast Asiatic peoples into Alaska and Canada from about 60,000 to 30,000 years ago. In that period of extended glaciation the sea level was much lower than at present, and east Siberia and Alaska formed a coherent landmass. The new arrivals could follow ice-free valleys, such as the Mackenzie Valley, down into regions with a milder climate and high plains where big game was plentiful. The immigrants penetrated deeper and deeper into the American continent, and at least by about 8000 B.C.E. they had moved from the northern extreme of North America to the southernmost tip of South America, the stormy sounds of Tierra del Fuego.

Who were these early invaders, the ancestors of the American Indian tribes? In all likelihood they were an offshoot of a proto-Mongoloid population in the northeastern part of Asia. Their exact ties with later linguistic stocks and archaeological remains in Asia have not been discovered so far, but their cultural heritage in North America seems to indicate that they were part of the rather uniform **circumpolar** and **circumboreal** culture that stretched from Scandinavia across northern Russia to Siberia. It is not surprising that the religious features of the historically related peoples in this broad culture are almost identical. Thus, hunting taboos, **animal ceremonialism**, beliefs in spirits, and **shamanism** have been common to such geographically distant peoples as the Saamis

(Lapps) of northern Europe and the Samoyeds of northern Asia as well as the Algonkian Indians of eastern Canada. Even myths and mythical motifs have their counterparts in Old World and New World circumpolar religions. Seen in an evolutionary context, the circumpolar stratum clearly contains the beginnings of religion in aboriginal North America.[1]

The immigration of these groups to America took place over several thousand years. The last to arrive from northeast Asia were probably the Athapascan Indians who now occupy western Canada and Alaska, but who also may have filtered down into the Southwest where their late descendants are the Apache and Navajo. The Athapascans are probably related to the Sino-Tibetan linguistic stock and may have carried with them religious ideas and rituals predating Chinese sacred kingship and Tibetan lamaism. Their original ideology was a religion of the hunters, modified by matrilinear customs such as girls' puberty rites.

The general picture of the northern Asian origins of Native Americans is clouded by the lack of precise knowledge of exactly when and how particular groups moved to certain areas and how they came to share certain cultural features while developing other distinctive ones. For example, one feature that appears to have remained relatively consistent throughout much of the Americas is the original hunting religion brought with the first immigrants to North America. However, there remain many intriguing and unanswered questions about the origins of various cultures and their relationships to other cultures. One interesting case is the speculation concerning the origins of the **totem poles** of the Northwest Coast Indians, which have been compared to ceremonial poles found in the cultures of the South Pacific as well as among the Maori of New Zealand. Some scholars have argued that the similarity among these cultural objects points to a common Pacific origin, but most American anthropologists reject these arguments. It is just as likely that totem poles (or myths showing similarity to Polynesian mythology) developed in North America independent of an origin or influence from the Pacific area.

The discussion of a trans-Pacific source of some religious traits becomes more relevant when we consider the origins of agricultural religious ideology, because of the more obvious parallels between the agricultural rituals of the Old World and those of the New World.

In contrast to the preservation of hunting life in the northern and southern extremities of the two Americas (doubtless for climatic reasons), from about 5000 B.C.E. the temperate and tropical areas of the Americas developed maize and manioc horticulture. Anthropologists are in general agreement about the indigenous origins and development of agriculture in America, but the picture is complicated by the fact that the American religious ideas and rituals related to agriculture are very similar to those in the Old World. Indeed, the same tales about agricultural spirits appear in both hemispheres. One example is the American story of the Corn Maiden, whose departure from the human world causes the disappearance of vegetable food but whose return to this world after a long absence results in abundant crops. This is a remarkable parallel to the myth of the flight and return of the fertility goddess in Europe and the Middle East. However, it is possible to argue that this tale simply depicts the passing of the seasons of the agricultural year and could have originated independently in both hemispheres. But whatever the ultimate origin or origins of Native American agriculture, a religious pattern associated with horticulture spread over northern South America and southern North America.

The end result of the long history of migration of peoples and development of cultures in both of the American continents is the existence of two contrasting religious orientations: the old hunting religions and the new horticultural religions. In general these two patterns can be characterized by two sets of features:

Hunting Pattern	*Horticultural Pattern*
Animal ceremonialism	Rain and fertility ceremonies
Quest for spiritual power	Priestly ritual
Male Supreme Being	Goddesses and gods
Annual ceremony of cosmic rejuvenation	Yearly round of fertility rites
Few stationary cult places	Permanent shrines and temples
Shamanism	**Medicine society** ritualism
Life after death beyond the horizon or in the sky	Life after death in the underworld or among the clouds

Of course each of these two patterns is only an ideal model. Every Native American tribe has its own emphasis on one pattern or the other or in many cases a distinctive blending of the two patterns. Our sketch of Shoshoni religion and Zuni religion will illustrate two "typical" cases of these two kinds of religious orientations.

The Formation of Religious Traditions

Native American religious traditions took shape in a manner somewhat different from world religions such as Christianity and Islam. Of course, all religious traditions are based in part on the previous religious heritage. For example, the formation of Christianity is not comprehensible without knowledge of Judaism, the Old Testament, Gnosticism, and Hellenism; similarly, Islam is not comprehensible without knowledge of pre-Islamic customs, Judaism, Syrian Christianity, and Manichaeism. Even though religions such as Christianity and Islam are established by founders—Jesus and Muhammad—as distinctively "new" religions, they still preserve elements of the preexisting religious situation. All religions tend to be conservative, because their sacred authority lies in the sanctity of the past: a myth records the sacred origin of a ritual, a legend explains the acquisition of a sacred object, a tradition preserves the account of a god's message to humans. At the same time, most religions remain open to the personal experiences of the spiritual world. The balance between faithfulness to tradition and openness to new experience is what constitutes the religious life.

A major difference between the formation of world religions such as Christianity and Islam, on the one hand, and Native American traditions, on the other, is that these world religions were established by particular founders and preserved as literary traditions, whereas Native American religions were handed down by tribes as oral traditions. In general the weight of the past—the emphasis on preserving the "letter" of the written record, such as Christianity's conformity to the Bible and Islam's conformity to the Qur'an (Koran)—is much heavier within written traditions than within oral traditions. Of course, oral traditions can and indeed have been passed down through many generations for long periods of time, among Native Americans as well as many other peoples. In native North America, oral traditions were the only means of transmitting beliefs and practices until the beginning of the nineteenth century, when the Cherokee tribe developed an alphabet and wrote down some of their heritage. Toward the end of the last century Indians increasingly entered missionary schools and came to read and write English, but still they tended to maintain their sacred traditions through oral transmission.

This major dependence on oral traditions has meant that native Indian religions have not been so dogmatically bound by what was handed down from the past. Over the whole continent, with the exception of parts of the Southwest, it was common for a person to enter into direct contact with the supernatural powers and receive their directions and personal protection. New cults and new ritual songs were introduced by the supernatural beings in visions and dreams. Native religion was thus quite charismatic and innovative, modifying and even replacing older traditions with new revelations. Probably no other cultures have given visions such importance in daily religious life as those of native North America.

Native American religions are formed through the interaction of preserving the prior tradition and at the same time accepting new visions. Old traditions, such as the Sun Dance of the Plains Indians, have been changed through visions, and visions have given rise to new traditions, as seen in the origin legends of the **medicine bundles** in eastern North America. While it is true that the New World preserves many old mythical accounts that connect it with Eurasia, such as the myths of the Flood and the **Mythic Twins** (described below), the visionary reformulations of some of these myths have often made them very different from their Old World counterparts. The origin of some rituals and practices is found in mythical accounts; other rituals and practices are authoritative because they were revealed in the visionary experiences of heroes in ages past— often experiences during situations of social and economic difficulty.

This explains the manifold and complex character of many American Indian traditions. On the Plains and in the Midwest not only tribes and clans but also families have their special oral traditions. For instance, among the Winnebago each clan has its own myth of the origin of the world, and each of these myths deviates from the others. In the same fashion, among Southwest Indians different clans of the same **pueblo** may perform the same ritual, but with significant variations. It seems that the authority for a myth or ritual does not rest in a fixed tradition as such but in the revelation of supernatural beings who are the ultimate source of all religious traditions.

Although there is considerable variation to mythical accounts and ritual practices, some have persisted as important patterns in Native American religious history. Among customs preserved from remote hunting times we find the **bear ceremonialism,** a continuous tradition of beliefs, myths, and rituals centered on the bear and practiced by a whole range of cultures from the Lapps (Saamis) of northern Europe to the Lenape (Delawares) along the Atlantic coast of North America. Bear ceremonialism involves the ritual appeasement and ceremonial disposal of a slain bear so that other bears will feel honored to be caught and killed. The ritual may be performed for other game animals as well (and was probably originally meant for all game animals killed). This animal ceremonialism is perhaps the most characteristic complex of hunting religion practiced in both America and the Old World. It is part of circumpolar culture and seems to go back to Paleolithic times in the Old World. In North America the best example of this complex is found among the Algonkian Indians of eastern Canada and the United States, who are known as the greatest preservers of old circumboreal religion. However, there are traces of animal ceremonialism throughout the religions of North America, including those in California and the Southwest. Remains of the old bear ceremonialism may be found even in the Pueblo Southwest.[2]

Another pattern of myths and beliefs at least partially deriving from Old World accounts is the Mythic Twins, or Dual Creators. This theme appears in two forms: the incipient dualism (or tension) between the Supreme Being and the **culture hero** or **trickster;** and the dualism between two world-ordering culture heroes.

The former theme of dualism is discernible in most parts of North America and implies a rivalry in mythical times between a divine figure (usually identified with the Supreme Being who is prominent in prayer and ritual) and the culture hero who only appears in mythology (and does not play a role in ritual). In essence the two represent similar functions, and in some places, for instance California, the culture hero (usually **Coyote**) is at the same time conceived as a Supreme Being. In the majority of tribes, however, there is a clear distinction between the two personages associated with their abilities as creators: the main Creator stands for the beneficial and complete creations and the culture hero takes care of lesser tasks (such as the founding of cultural and religious institutions) or makes less beneficial or ambiguous contributions to creation (such as the introduction of death). The culture hero's failures turn him into a comic figure, a trickster. As an egotistical and obscene trickster, this character has given rise to the largest and most important part of American Indian mythology, the trickster cycle.[3] The culture hero and trickster came to be seen as having an evil disposition when the opposition between the two divine figures was overlaid with the more pronounced dualism between the Dual Creators, an Asiatic theme that was spread through North America (along with the Earthdiver Myth). However, the evilness belongs only to the mythological figure and has not turned American religions into dualistic ethic traditions.

In its second form the Mythic Twins theme is connected with the twin culture heroes, one a positive transformer of the landscape and founder of institutions, the other one a destructive and unfriendly being. We find this cycle of tales primarily represented in certain horticultural milieus such as among the Pueblos of the Southwest and the Iroquois of the Northeast. Secondarily this theme has also spread to the neighboring nonfarming peoples like the Navajo. A separate widespread myth, the Star Husband Tale, makes the divine twins the children of a heavenly god and the goddess of vegetation.

Another prominent pattern of Native American religion, found among horticultural peoples in the South, is the mythical account in which the cosmic beginning was not focused on the creation of the world but on the emergence of the first human beings from the interior of the earth. There is mention of four or five worlds, one on top of the other, through which the first humans climbed, with the aid of a vine or a tree (probably the **World Tree**). Each of the worlds had its own color but was generally dark. The last world into which the first humans arrived is the present world, and the hole through which they emerged is the navel of the world. As we shall see later, it is symbolized in the sacred **sipapu** hollow of the Pueblo cult chamber. This is the **Emergence Myth,** diffused over the southern and horticultural Indian areas of the United States. It is easy to see that the appearance of humans on earth is here paralleled with the rise of the plants from the earth's interior.

These three widespread patterns—animal ceremonialism, the Mythic Twins (or Dual Creators), and the Emergence Myth—help illustrate the nature of religion among Native Americans. These patterns are directly related to religious patterns of northern Europe and Asia and came to be disseminated over most of the American continent. However, unlike the founded traditions of Christianity and Islam, Native American religions were not linked directly to particular founders and restricted by bodies of doctrine until the rise of Indian religious movements inspired by Christianity, especially in the nineteenth century. Native American religions developed very freely, bound only by the limits of the natural setting, social structure, and general cultural patterns.

CHAPTER II

Native American Religions: An Overview

There are so many Native American religions and their expressions are so varied that it is difficult to generalize upon all Native American religions. As we shall see in Chapters III and IV, the religious life of the Shoshoni and that of the Zuni Indians show amazing diversity between two North American tribal groups and even a large amount of variation within each group. Nevertheless, if we keep in mind the distinctive religious differences of individual tribes, some general features are found among most groups. For example, we have already seen that there are two basic patterns of a hunting culture and a farming culture throughout the Americas, with each tribe emphasizing one or the other pattern or a blending of the two patterns. Some other general features can be isolated in the religions of North American Indians, with greater or lesser emphasis depending on the particular group.

Four prominent features in North American Indian religions are a similar worldview, a shared notion of cosmic harmony, emphasis on experiencing directly powers and visions, and a common view of the cycle of life and death. These features will be treated separately, but it is useful to provide an initial identification of each. Worldview is the total understanding of life and the universe held by a particular people or culture. North American Indians have worldviews that in many respects are remarkably similar, particularly in the way they perceive the interrelationship of humans and animals. Many North American Indians also share a notion of cosmic harmony, in which humans, animals, plants, all of nature, and even supernatural figures cooperate to bring about a balanced and harmonious universe. North American Indian traditions emphasize a direct experience of spiritual power through dreams and visions; as we have already seen, the sacredness and prestige of these striking revelations often results in the modification or replacement of previous traditional elements. Native Americans have a common view of time as a recurring cycle; they are interested mainly in how this cycle affects people in this life and have only a vague notion of another existence after death.

Worldview

If we want to grasp the essential character of North American Indian religions it is natural to start with their worldview. Worldview is a concept that may be interpreted in different ways. The American anthropologist Robert Redfield defines worldview as "the way a people characteristically look outward upon the universe,"[4] and it may be convenient to apply that definition here. In our context worldview then stands for a people's concept of existence and their view of the universe and its powers.

Most North American Indians consider that human existence was designed by the creator divinities at the time of the "first beginning." Mythological tales report that in those days all beings on earth were more or less human, but a change took place that turned many primeval beings into animals and birds. Only those who today are human beings retained their forms. Because of this genesis there is still today a close affinity between people and animals: they are brothers, and it is people's task to respect and be in harmony with the animals. It is interesting that domesticated animals such as dogs have not been included in this brotherhood, whereas domesticated horses have. Indeed, on the Plains there is even a cult of the horse. It is difficult to tell whether the fact that the horse is of foreign, European origin has contributed to its lofty position. In the main, however, it is the wild, independent animals to which Native Americans' religious attention has been paid. All over the Americas they have been thought to manifest the mysterious qualities of existence.

One consequence of the close kinship between humans and animals has been the tendency for Native Americans to imitate the animals in dress, actions, and projective thought. The feather-lined shirts, the feather ornaments for dancing, and the feather plumes in the hair of the American Indians are all measures to instill the capacities of birds (spirit birds) in the human being. Some feather arrangements in the hair seem to have obtained a secondary meaning—marking the number of enemies killed, success in scalping an enemy, or other deeds. The Mandan and their neighbors near the Upper Missouri developed the large war bonnets with a row of feathers in a headband, trailing down the back; these were more a symbol of dignity and intrepidity than of spiritual assistance—although the latter possibility cannot be excluded. These war bonnets were then later adopted by other Indians. The feather decorations of American Indians remind us of those of the Siberian **shaman,** which is a further testimony of the spiritual background of the "feather complex." Apparently feathers manifest spiritual essence, particularly of beings on high.

The bond between animals and humans is also expressed in ritual activities. Plains Indian dances in which the men imitate the movements of buffaloes or wear their horns and skins are supposed to bring forth this valuable game. They are not, as earlier research took for granted, magic rituals to multiply the animals. They are rather acts of supplication in which Indians, by imitating the wild, express their desires and expectations. Such a ritual tells us of the Indian's veneration for the active powers of the universe: it is a prayer.

The final consequence of Native Americans' close affinity to the animals is **animalism,** that is, the concept of spirits as animals. This is a characteristic feature in North American Indian religions. Of course, wherever hunting cultures are to be found, supernatural beings come dressed in animal attire. In North America, however, the vision complex, of which more will be said shortly, has strengthened and perpetuated the belief in animal spirits.

Here we may well ask whether we should speak about "animal spirits" or "spirit animals." The former term may indicate either the notion of spirits in animal form or the concept of the spirits—or souls—of animals. The latter term suggests that some animals may not be real animals, but spirits. In North American traditions both designations seem to apply, because the boundary between animals and spirits here is very vague. Therefore, both terms will be used in the following.

Indians think that animals are by nature mysterious since their behavior is both similar and different to that of humans. Such a tension between known and understood and unknown and not understood usually creates a sentiment of something uncanny, something not quite belonging to normal reality. The Ojibway of the Great Lakes think that, although most stones are not alive, some are. They can be seen rolling of their own accord, and a **medicine man** or a **medicine woman** can talk to them and receive their answers. Apparently, stones are divided according to their possession or lack of mysterious qualities. A similar rule holds for animals. All bears are mysterious in their various ways, but some bears are more mysterious than others, being able to talk or change forms (as experienced in dreams and visions). The former bears are in spite of everything ordinary bears, the latter are spirits. However, sometimes it is difficult to find out which category of bears Indian informants are referring to.

We are here reminded of the fact that to Native American religious thinking there is a dividing line between what belongs to the ordinary or natural world around us and what belongs to the supernatural or spiritual world. In some scholarly quarters it has been denied that any such categorization exists among the Indians, or it has been said that it only occurs among those Indians who have been touched by Christianity. However, a consideration of all the evidence makes it quite clear that in their spontaneous experience of religious miracles and in some cases in their thinking about such experiences and existence as such, Indians distinguish between an ordinary and a spiritual world. It is difficult for us to pinpoint which things belong to either category. As mentioned above, a bear may be an ordinary animal, or it may represent the shape of a supernatural being. To some tribes certain mountains are supernatural, to others they are not.

Indeed, some natural phenomena and cultural objects are so saturated with supernaturalness that they are set aside from all other things. They are sacred and therefore dangerous, **taboo.** For instance, the Indians surrounding Yellowstone Park feared its spouting geysers. Their eruptions were thought to spring from the operations of capricious spirits. Archaeological evidence seems to suggest that the Indians may have offered axes and other implements to the underground spirits. Otherwise, however, they avoided the dangerous spots. There are many other examples of the distinction between natural and supernatural. Plains Indians received in visions spirit instructions to leave alone certain tools or abstain from certain actions. The sacred Arapaho flatpipe cannot be touched except under proper ritual conditions. It is preserved in a special lodge and carefully wrapped up in blankets. One Shoshoni medicine man refused to dine with me at a restaurant because his spirit had forbidden him to eat with cutlery. Whoever transgresses such taboo rules runs the risk of becoming sick or paralyzed, or even dying. That person will bring misery and misfortune not only to himself, family, and kin, but to the whole community.

Some Indian pronouncements sound as if the whole universe, particularly the natural environment, is sacred. This is not so; if it were, Indians would not point out certain stones, mountains, and lakes as sacred. Conservationists have mistakenly assumed that Indians are ecologists because they supposedly care for all of nature. In fact, there are many proofs of the devastation of nature by Indians.[5] However, Indians have paid more attention to nature than perhaps any other peoples, and Indian hunters have tended to protect nature, or parts of nature, as a manifestation of the supernatural. They care about the trees, because they give evidence of the supernatural; they care about the animals, because they may represent spirits; they care about the vast lands, because they may reveal God. Nature is potentially sacred, or rather, it turns into sacred matter when humans experience the supernatural in vision, meditation, or ritual.

There has been no remarkable speculation on the relations between the natural world and the spiritual world in the Indian worldview. Perhaps one could say that for the Indians the spiritual reveals the true nature of the ordinary world around us, but this inference should not be emphasized. The Western religious dichotomy between a world of spiritual plenitude and a world of material imperfection, a dualism pertaining to Christian and Gnostic doctrines, has no counterpart in American Indian thinking. Indians value highly life on earth, and their religion supports their existence in this world. The whole spirit of their religion is one of harmony, vitality, and appreciation of the world around them.

Perhaps the Western concept of "nature" is too narrow to use in this connection. Nature, the world, and the universe are concepts that flow into each other in Indian consciousness. What some scholars describe as "nature rituals" Indians view as affecting the whole of the universe. The Sun Dance is not just a ritual that promotes the vegetation and animal life during the new year that it introduces, it is a recapitulation of the creation; in fact, it is creation and its effects concern the whole evolution and sustenance of the universe.

The universe is usually divided into three levels—heaven, earth, and underworld, a division that is a heritage from ancient times and is also known in northern Eurasia. However, there are some variations in this world picture. The Bella Coola of British Columbia believe that there are five worlds on top of each other, of which ours is the middle one. Many Pueblo peoples of the Southwest believe in the existence of four underworlds and four upper worlds, and the Navajo have taken over their idea of the four subterranean realms, one over the other.

The various worlds are often united through the World Tree, which has its roots in the underworld, stretches through the world of humans and animals, and has its crown in the sky world. The World Tree is represented by such ritual structures as the Sun Dance post (which is an uprooted tree) or the Omaha sacred pole. The three levels of the universe are marked on the Sun Dance post: the eagle at its top manifests the sky world, the buffalo skull on its trunk or at its base is the world of animals and humans, and the offerings of tobacco and water on the earth close to the base, destined for Mother Earth, symbolize the relations to the underworld. The myths of the tree or vine on which the ancestors climbed up from the underworld(s), according to Southwestern Indians, also remind us of the idea of the World Tree.

In myths and rituals the sacred areas of the supernatural powers are drawing close to people. They may become identical with the areas people occupy today. Thus, the mythic world of the Navajo supernatural beings is situated between the four sacred mountains that enclose the central country of the Navajo people: Big Sheep Peak in the north, Pelado Mountain in the east, Mount Taylor in the south, and the San Francisco Peaks in the west. To take another example, the Shoshonean myths portray a landscape in the Great Basin that still is the home of many Shoshoni groups today.

The supernatural powers that govern the universe are multifarious. There is usually a heavenly god who rules over the sky, a host of spirits who control the atmospheric powers, an innumerable crowd of spirits who influence human life on earth, and also some beings, including Mother Earth, who roam the nether world. Very often these spirits, or a large number of them, are conceived as a unity. This unity may consist of a collectivity of spirits or of a Supreme Being (usually identified with the sky god) supervising or taking in the functions of various spiritual powers. On the Plains, both these concepts may exist side by side. Thus **Wakan Tanka** of the Lakota Sioux is a term comprehending a set of spirits from different levels, functions, and areas—sixteen all together. (The number is the speculation of holy men.) However, it is also the name of a personal god, the quintessence of all powers. To one Lakota division, the Oglala Lakota, the concept of *Wakan Tanka* swings between the two poles of unity and collectivity.

Psychologically seen, the two cognitive elaborations represent two ways of looking at the supernatural. When people perceive the universe as a unit, whole and indivisible, the figure of the single godhead stands in focus. When human attention is drawn to the particular acts of the divine, such as thunder, food giving, and healing, particular powers appear that express the activities referred to. The Supreme Being fades into the background, unless he is especially bound up with one of these activities. There is thus a tension between universalism and particularism in the concepts of the supernatural and the universe.

The worldview of North American Indians reveals a concept of existence contrasting sharply with that of the Western world and the Judeo-Christian tradition. There is no sharp differentiation between divinity and humans, nor is there a clear distinction between humans and animals. Not only is there a different relationship between these beings, but also the beings themselves are viewed in a distinctive fashion calling for their own terms. The Western world focuses on one divinity as "God," but Native Americans, although they have the notion of a Supreme Being, emphasize an abundance of "powers" and "spirits." These powers are not far removed from humans but interact freely with humans, especially in dreams and visions (as will be seen later in this chapter). Some animals are spirits, as some spirits are animals. In general, the Native American view of "nature" is much more alive and filled with spiritual activity than the Western view of nature. The Native American worldview can in some instances be characterized as emphasizing cosmic harmony.

Cosmic Harmony

Today's Indians often emphasize the unitary, balanced system of the universe as made up of humans, animals, trees and plants, nature as a whole, and the supernaturals. For instance, Jackson Beardy, a modern Cree Indian artist, sees the world as a unit dominated by the sacred number four. He told me that the world has four basic elements: air, water, fire, and stone. The creation took place in four processes: the creation of the earth, the plants, the animals, and the human beings. There are four basic colors in the universe; and so on. Now, this is scarcely the original worldview of the artist's people, the Woodland Cree of Manitoba, because Canadian Woodland Indians are not known to have such concepts. It is rather a worldview that has striking resemblances with the cosmic speculations of Plains and Pueblo Indians. As a matter of fact, when questioned, Jackson Beardy admitted that he had absorbed ideas from the Plains Indians, the Northwest Coast Indians, and other Indians. He is convinced that there are no real differences between Indian religions, only different names.

The same position is taken today by most young Indians who believe in **Pan-Indianism;** that is, they consider that all Native American tribes basically share the same culture and the same religion and they want to revert to this culture and religion. They present a "North American religion" as an integrated system of beliefs and rituals with fixed symbolism, the same for all tribes. This is, however, a late idea,·formed under the pressure of white domination. Still, its foundation, the concept of cosmic harmony, a harmony in which living beings also take part, is much older. It is an outgrowth of the speculations among priests in predominantly agrarian societies where religious ideas, natural phenomena, humans, and other beings have been drawn together as parallels, analogues, and symbols in a connected religio-philosophical pattern. Certainly, the very germs of this speculation may be retraced to the ancient hunting milieu. However, it is particularly in the horticultural milieu with its developed and intricate ritualism, its grandiose mythology, and speculating priest-thinkers that the idea of cosmic harmony is really at home.

To show the uniqueness of this ideology we may here contrast the thought systems of a hunting tribe like the Naskapi of Labrador and a horticultural group like the Tewa of New Mexico. The Naskapi, says an expert on their religion, Frank G. Speck, do not classify their religious ideas. "For a system is scarcely to be expected to appear on the surface as covering the aggregation of metaphysical ideas so rudimentary as those exhibited in Montagnais-Naskapi thought. . . . That any conception of categories is alien to the thought of the people must be apparent to anyone who has viewed their undisciplined life."[6] On the other hand, there is an unconscious thought system that sometimes has a ring of Platonism, because earthly forms are seen as having their supernatural ideal forms. Each animal species has its master (lord, boss); this **master of the animals** is usually conceived as a mysterious animal spirit larger than ordinary animals of the same kind. Thus, the giant beaver who governs the beavers decides their allotment as game food to the hunters and their return to the world after death. The fish also have a master, but he is identified with the moose-fly, strangely enough. The principle remains, however: living beings have their supernatural guardians. In the case of humans, it is the Supreme Being who plays the superior role.

This simple system of the hunters contrasts with the rich symbolism of the agricultural Tewa, a Pueblo tribe in New Mexico described in detail in an excellent work by a Tewa (San Juan) Indian scholar, Alfonso Ortiz. The Tewa are organized in two **ceremonial moieties** or halves that are responsible in particular for the rituals of the calendar. These rituals regulate the seasons and serve the supernatural cosmic system. Whereas in the inchoate religion of the Naskapi the supernatural beings stand out as the powers who decide the course of events, in the Tewa worldview they are part of the ritual machinery, impersonated in the rituals by members of the moiety divisions. It is the cooperation between the two moieties that brings together the wholeness of Tewa existence. A symbol of this wholeness is the sacred center, the navel of the Earth Mother, a keyhole-shaped arrangement of stones on the southern plaza. Late in the winter seeds are placed in this navel to symbolize the reawakening of nature. From this navel the world is oriented. The world has four quarters, and so has its ritual manifestation on earth, the pueblo.

The complementary powers of the universe are contained in the two moieties, which represent summer and winter and are protected by the Blue Corn Mother and the White Corn Mother, respectively.

The summer moiety is particularly associated with the furthering of vegetation, the winter moiety with the furthering of hunting. Moreover, the moieties are combined with symbolic colors, the summer moiety with black (for clouds), green (for crops), and yellow (for sunshine), the winter moiety with white (for winter moisture) and red (for warfare and hunting). As a consequence of this division, the summer moiety stands for femaleness and the winter moiety for maleness. The summer moiety impersonates in its rituals the gods from the warm south, the winter moiety the gods from the cold north. In this way everything that exists is divided up between the ceremonial moieties.[7]

There are also secret societies belonging to the moieties or balancing between them. In the annual cycle of rituals (called "works") these societies perform retreats and prayer sessions associated with the progression of the year and its economic activities. "The intent of each work is to harmonize man's relations with the spirits, and to insure that the desired cyclical changes will continue to come about in nature."[8]

Why is there this difference in outlook between the Naskapi and the Tewa? One reason is certainly the wide differences in their conditions of existence. In their hard struggle in an Arctic environment the Naskapi, strewn over the country in small hunting camps, had few possibilities and few incentives to create bodies of speculative thought and little ritualism that made such speculation necessary. The agricultural, closely connected Tewa Indians, inhabiting a circumscribed pueblo and living in a more pleasant climate, had enough surplus time to consider their affinity with the universe. The picture of this universe was taken from their own cultural structure. Their dualistic cosmology may, as Ortiz suggests, have been stimulated by a dual subsistence system (hunting and horticulture). In a wider perspective their thought system is part of a Pueblo Indian philosophy that may go back to tendencies in archaic American Indian thinking.

Powers and Visions

The Jesuit missionaries of the 1630s who had arrived in the area of the Great Lakes to convert the Indians there were astonished to find religions so different in structure and expression from their own Catholic faith. "Their superstitions are infinite," wrote Father de Brébeuf on the Huron, an Iroquoian people, and Father Francois du Perron made the following statement: "All their actions are dictated to them directly by the devil, who speaks to them now in the form of a crow or some similar bird, now in the form of a flame or a ghost, and all this in dreams, to which they show great deference. They consider the dream as the master of their lives; it is the God of the country. It is this which dictates to them their feasts, their hunting, their fishing, their war, their trade with the French, their remedies, their dances, their games, their songs."[9]

Behind these theological comments we have here the earliest Western descriptions of the role that dreams and visions have played in Native American religion. All over North America, with exception of the Southwest, spiritual power has come to people in their dreams or in visions they have received in isolated places in the wilderness. Indeed, it is possible to say that the **vision quest** is the most characteristic feature of North American religions outside the Pueblo area. For the lone hunter safety and success depended on the guardian spirit acquired through the vision quest. The guardian spirit was closer at hand than the high god or other spirits. The connection between a person and a protective spirit could become so intense that the person took part in the spirit's qualities and even in its life. In northern Mexico, this close bond is called **nagualism,** after the Indian term *nagual* (the guardian animal that is the individual's second ego). When the spirit died (and spirits could die), the person also succumbed.

The relationship to a guardian spirit through vision is evidence of the importance of spiritual contact in American Indian religion. Indians "believe" when they see or feel the supernatural being. A historical document from the seventeenth-century Southwest illustrates this point. The Spanish missionary Fray Alonso de Benavides tells us how he was visited by a Jicarilla Apache chieftain who much admired his altar and was informed that God was on that altar. However, the Apache was not satisfied, for God was not visible on the altar. When he left he was very disappointed, for he wished to have seen God. In Indian religion, the vision quest provided an opportunity for direct contact with the supernatural.

The basic vision quest in North America is connected with puberty or the years immediately preceding puberty. The young boy (girls do not usually participate in the vision quest) is required to seek the assistance of a guardian spirit to withstand the trials of existence and have luck in hunting, warfare, love, and so on. The parents or elders send him out, usually together with other boys, into the forest or mountains to fast and suffer from the cold and the attacks of dangerous wild animals. In his weakened state he may have a vision of the spirit that henceforth becomes his guardian spirit. (There are many cases told of supplicants who were not blessed by spirits.) This quest, which we may call the "**puberty quest**," was transformed into a quest for full-grown men on the Plains and in parts of adjacent territories. On the Plains the warriors repeatedly withdrew into the wilderness to seek spirits. A Plains Indian may therefore have a variety of guardian spirits, each of which is good for a different purpose.

Consequently, the boundary line between common visionaries and medicine men has been very slight among Plains Indians (medicine women will be discussed later). One can say that in comparison with ordinary Indians medicine men have more spirits, and their spirits are specialized to help cure the diseases of their clients. The medicine man receives his mission to cure from the spirits that come to him, and in his visions he receives instructions in the ways of doctoring.

The most common therapeutic method is to remove the agent of the disease, whether it be an object or a spirit. Sucking, blowing, and drawing it out (with a feather fan) are the most common techniques. In some areas, and particularly along the Northwest Coast, the medicine man falls into a trance or ecstasy to enable his soul to transcend the boundaries to the other world. In his trance he gathers information from the spirits of the dead, or even steals away the soul of a patient that has gone to the realm of the dead during the feverish coma of its owner. The medicine man then brings the soul back to the sick person, usually by pressing his hands against the latter's crown. Such a medicine man who falls recurringly into a deep trance to save a person's life is called a **shaman.**

Shamans, however, are not only doctors. They are able to divine the whereabouts of game, the location of a missing person, and the course of future events. Among the Athapascans of the Southwest (Apache and Navajo) the shaman goes into a trance to find out the nature of the disease before other medicine men start their doctoring.

Common visionaries, medicine men, and shamans all have their authority from spiritual revelations in visions. As said before, this direct contact with the supernatural world through visions means more to American Indians outside of the Pueblo area than the knowledge of supernatural powers through traditional lore. Sometimes spiritual revelation comes not through the sought vision, but in a spontaneous dream, particularly among the Iroquois in New York State and the Mohave in western Arizona and southern California. The Iroquois decide their actions from interpretations of dreams, and the Mohave even dream their myths, that is, construct their myths on the basis of dream contents. Medicine men and shamans west of the Rocky Mountains receive their powers not through the vision quest, but through spontaneous dreams and visions.

Since time immemorial Indian shamans have facilitated their contacts with the supernatural through potent psychotropic drugs, drugs that affect consciousness and behavior. Tobacco is a well known and important ingredient in American Indian rituals. In the Eastern Woodlands and on the Plains, the smoking of a pipe introduces most ceremonies and most peace talks. There is reasonable evidence to suggest that in bygone times the pipe without the bowl functioned as a suction instrument through which the shaman could both remove a disease object from a patient and intoxicate himself with tobacco fumes.

Many psychotropic plants have been used for the attainment of trance states. Datura was used in California, the Southwest, and the Southeast. In recent times peyote, the small spineless cactus, plays a similar role. A whole religion has grown up around peyote, particularly on the Plains. (This subject will be further discussed in Chapter III.)

The Cycle of Life and Death

In contrast to those in Western cultures, Native Americans conceive of time not in a linear, but in a cyclical form. Western time concepts include a beginning and an end; American Indians understand time as an eternally recurring cycle of events and years. Some Indian languages lack terms for the past and the future; everything is resting in the present. This explains to us how mythical events apparently thought to have happened long ago may repeat themselves in present ritual occurrences. The Lakota define the year as a circle around the border of the world. The circle is a symbol of both the earth (with its encircling horizons) and time. The changes of sunup and sundown around the horizon during the course of the year delineate the contours of time, time as a part of space.[10] An illustration of this way of counting time is indicated in stone arrangements on mountaintops and plateaus in the Rocky Mountains: the stones are laid in a wide circle around a central hub, and the place of the summer solstice is marked. The "**medicine wheels,**" as these stone structures are called, served as some sort of calendars, among other things.

The cyclical time concept applies not only to the macrocosmos, the world and the year's rhythm, but also to the microcosmos, the human being. Each person makes a cycle of time from birth to death. Rituals mark the important changes of life: birth ceremonies, puberty rituals, initiation rites into tribal societies, and death rituals. The cyclical concept demands that death is not an end, but a beginning of new life, either on this earth (**reincarnation** as another human or **transmigration** into some animal, most often an owl) or in a transcendent hereafter. Very often one individual might hold several ideas about the dead at the same time: the dead as residing in the other world, the dead as reincarnated in other persons, and the dead as haunting ghosts. This may appear to be a logical inconsistency in Indian thinking, but it should not be so considered. Different situations call for different interpretations of the fate of humans after death. (And in fact Western people themselves do not reconcile their apparent inconsistencies on the fate of individuals following death.)

Native Americans usually avoided the issue of death, thinking that nothing could be known with certainty about the state of the dead. The question of a person's survival after his or her demise has never been a prominent theme for American Indian speculation (although the Jesuit fathers thought so). As said before, religion in aboriginal America has always been in the service of life, not death. Beliefs about the dead are abstruse, vague, and of little consequence. The best descriptions there are emanate from shamans who have gone beyond life to liberate sick people's souls entrapped by the dead. These descriptions tell us much about the difficult roads to the other world and the obstacles to be met. With Paul Radin we may say that these tales are folkloristically reworked, rich in detail, but scarcely meaningful to the ordinary person who primarily trusts his or her own religious experiences.[11] Conditions in the next life are not so well documented, although there are occasionally illuminating reports. These are usually modeled on the setting and conditions in this life and consequently vary with cultural background.

In popular contexts we often talk about the "happy hunting grounds." It has been said by some authorities that Indians never believed in them, but this is wrong. Hunting tribes usually think that there is a happy land after death, at least for those who have conformed to the norms of society. There is plenty of game in that land. Horticulturists tend to believe in a subterranean realm of the dead, the place of Mother Earth who produces the new life of vegetation. For obvious reasons this realm portrays a more gloomy picture of afterlife. However, often the horticulturists retain the old idea of a happy paradise, whatever its location, filled with the bounty of the earth. The question of whether there were different realms of the dead based on good and bad deeds in pre-Columbian Indian belief is difficult to answer. However, we know definitely that such ideas developed under the impact of Christianity, for cyclical thinking does not provide for a resuscitation of the dead in this life. As an Indian told me, those who are gone are gone forever. Only in religious movements that have been inspired by Christian ideas, such as the **Ghost Dance** around 1890, is the return of the dead possible.

The overview of Native American religions in this chapter provides us with a general understanding of the worldview, cosmic harmony, powers and visions, and the cycle of life and death so important to this religious heritage. But because this overview has attempted to characterize Native American religion as a whole, especially in North America, it has necessarily been quite general. The next two chapters offer more concrete description of the richness of two specific Native American traditions.

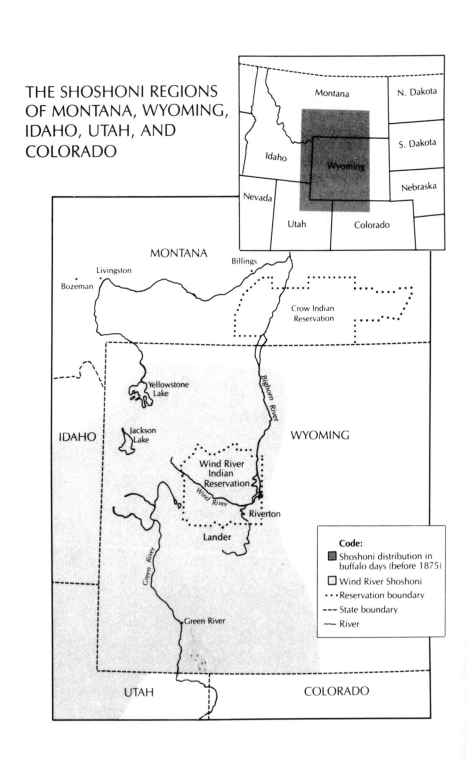

THE SHOSHONI REGIONS
OF MONTANA, WYOMING,
IDAHO, UTAH, AND
COLORADO

Montana

N. Dakota

Idaho

S. Dakota

Wyoming

Nevada

Nebraska

Utah

Colorado

MONTANA

Billings

Livingston

Bozeman

Crow Indian
Reservation

Yellowstone
Lake

Bighorn River

Jackson
Lake

IDAHO

WYOMING

Wind River
Indian
Reservation

Wind River

Riverton

Lander

Green River

Green River

Code:

Shoshoni distribution in
buffalo days (before 1875)

Wind River Shoshoni

• • • Reservation boundary

– – – State boundary

∿ River

UTAH

COLORADO

CHAPTER III

The Religion of the Wind River Shoshoni: Hunting, Power, and Visions

The richness and variety of Native American religions seen in the two previous chapters make it difficult to provide a general overview of so many complex and fascinating traditions. Limiting our focus to just one tribal group, the Wind River Shoshoni, at first glance may seem to simplify the interpretation of a Native American religious tradition. However, the full richness and diversity of Native American religions can be appreciated only when they are seen in the context of a particular tribal group.

The nature of every Native American religion is in sharp contrast to traditions such as the "founded" religions of Christianity, Islam, and Buddhism. These founded religions are organized around the experience of the founding figure; the scriptures record the life of the founder and the religious texts comment on this experience; the community of religious practice is drawn together as a following of the founder. Especially because these traditions became codified in writing by a professional religious leadership, it is rather easy to identify the formal "teaching" or "message" of these religions: for example, the Nicene Creed in Christianity, the Four Noble Truths of Buddhism, and the confession of faith in Allah and Muhammad (the Shahade) in Islam. Of course, the beliefs and practices of individual members of these religions are much more diverse than what is seen in these very formal statements, but this individual variation can be measured against the codified formal statement.

In a Native American religious tradition there is no single

founder, no scriptural authority, no specific "church" or religious organization, no professional religious leadership. Rather, religion has been handed down as an oral tradition from one generation to another. The tribal group itself is the total religious community that receives, modifies, and transmits the religious tradition to the next generation. Because they are oral traditions, they are not bound so closely to the "fixed" character of the written word and past precedent as seen in founded religions; and because Native American religions emphasize direct contact with supernatural beings in visions and dreams, these traditions have more readily been transformed by the powerful experiences of remarkable individuals. In short, the oral traditions of Native American religions are more fluid and vary more greatly among individual members of a tradition than is the case with most world religions.

Because there is no written creed or codified doctrine for Native American religions, we must observe the rituals practiced and listen to the myths and beliefs told by the members of a particular tribe to discover the tribe's worldview. By paying close attention to their beliefs and practices we will come to see their view of human life and the cosmos as a total world of meaning. As we saw in Chapter I, there are basically two kinds of religious orientation in Native American traditions, a hunting pattern and a horticultural pattern. In this chapter the religion of the Wind River Shoshoni is described and interpreted as an example of the hunting pattern; in the next chapter the religion of the Zuni will be treated as an example of the horticultural pattern. For each religion, we will look first at the historical conditions of its development, then explore more closely the religious beliefs and practices, and finally provide more detailed description of some examples of concrete religious life.

The Development of Shoshoni Culture and Religion

The Wind River Shoshoni are named after their reservation in the central western part of the state of Wyoming. Their land is a sagebrush plain intersected by the upper course of the Wind River and bordered by the Rocky Mountains on the west and the open short grass plains on the east. The Indians on the reservation, Shoshoni and Arapaho, have access both to the warm valleys of the river and the rich hunting grounds up in the mountains. This country was chosen as a reservation in 1868 by Chief Washakie, the famous leader of the Shoshoni for almost sixty years. Their former enemies, the Arapaho, an Algonkian Plains tribe, were transferred to the reservation ten years later. The two tribes kept apart from each other.

Before they were collected on the reservation, the ancestors of the present Wind River Shoshoni belonged to different Shoshonean groups. In a larger perspective they formed part of the widely spread Shoshonean population (known linguistically as Numic) that for many centuries had been at home in the semideserts of the Great Basin and southern California. The Basin Numic Indians, divided into many groups such as the Ute, Paiute, Chemehuevi, Gosiute, and so on, were seed and nut gatherers and hunters of small game. They had one of the most simple cultures in North America: they lived in wickiups (brushwood huts or brush shelters), had little social organization above the family level, spent much time traveling from one source of food to another, and held very elementary thanksgiving feasts with round dances. Their eastern offshoots are the Shoshoni of Wyoming and the Comanche of the southern Plains. Due to ecological and historical influences, the culture of these Indians changed considerably from their Basin heritage.

Because the Wind River Shoshoni religion is closely related to this complex cultural background, a description of their prereservation history is necessary. The majority of them were Plains Shoshoni, mounted warriors whose Basin culture had been partially overlayered by Plains culture from the eighteenth century. They hunted buffalo, lived in portable tents of buffalo skin (**tipis**), had a strict military organization under a powerful paramount chief, but at the same time kept a flexible band organization under lesser chiefs. They had societies for men, at least from the nineteenth century, and celebrated the Sun Dance as their great annual ceremony. However, in many respects they departed from the Plains cultural pattern as we know it among the Crow, Lakota, Kiowa, and Cheyenne, which was characterized by a more intricate social and ceremonial organization, more reliance on the buffalo for food, sole use of *tipis* for shelter, and a geometric art. For example, the Shoshoni groups, in addition to their use of the *tipi,* which was typical of the Plains, also built mat houses. They shared some crafts in common with Plains groups, such as a particular bead technique and rawhide work, but unlike the Plains Indians they also made baskets. When the buffalo hunting was over for the season the various bands and family groups spread among the foothill areas and along mountain rivers where they hunted deer, mountain sheep, and small game, fished, and gathered bulbs, berries, and wild plants—remnants of the old Basin way of living.

This style of mountain life was more typical for another group of Wyoming Shoshoni, the Sheepeaters. They were part of a small but widely spread out population in the mountain districts of Wyoming, Idaho, and Montana that had adapted itself to mountain conditions. Indeed, they owed their name to the fact that, more than other Shoshoni, they hunted the bighorn sheep. Their pattern of life was ancient Shoshonean, combined with such Plateau Indian features from the north as salmon and trout fishing in the mountain rivers. Until the 1860s they lacked horses and therefore were called "walkers." They lived in brush lodges and did not associate with other groups.

There were other Shoshoni groups in southwestern Wyoming, in the Bear River country. Originally representing a very simple Basin culture, they mixed with white trappers in the beginning of the nineteenth century and became traders on the active Fort Laramie–Fort Bridger–Salt Lake City trade route. They developed a culture of their own, part white, part Indian.

After the Indian wars of the nineteenth century, all these Shoshoni Indians (and half-breeds) were collected on reservations in Idaho (Lemni, Fort Hall) and Wyoming (Wind River). Because there has always been lively interaction among the various groups and much intermarriage, it is natural that some Wyoming Indians settled in Idaho, and some Idaho Indians in Wyoming. Another factor in the shifting of Shoshoni Indians was the moving of all the Yellowstone Park Sheepeaters to reservations in Idaho. However, the present Wind River Shoshoni are mainly descendants of former Wyoming Shoshoni.

This complex cultural and historical background is reflected in the makeup of Wind River Shoshoni religion as we know it during the present century. There is, first of all, the religious complex related to the culture of the hunters and gatherers manifested in hunting ideas, shamanism, and mythology. Second, there is the overlay of Plains ideas and ritualism represented by the vision quest, the Sun

Dance, an active high-god concept, and belief in a happy hunting ground after death. This restructuring of religion may have taken place between 1775 and 1825, possibly earlier, and was accompanied by a strong emphasis on war ceremonialism. Since the Plains Shoshoni were the dominant group in Wyoming's Shoshonean population, they also put a strong stamp on the religion of the Wind River Shoshoni in modern reservation times.

Nevertheless, about the time of the first settlement on the reservation and particularly in connection with the defeat of the militant Ghost Dance religion about 1890–1891, another reorientation of religion took place, this time in a more peaceful direction: beliefs and practices associated with war were discarded and there was a greater concern with health and happiness. This was the time when the traditional form of the vision quest was gradually abandoned and was even declared harmful to its participants; at the same time the Sun Dance was reinterpreted as a ritual for healing of diseases and for tribal coherence, and Christian symbolism and values penetrated traditional religion. The introduction of **Peyotism,** the peyote religion, dates from this period. (Peyote is a cactus that grows in Mexico and southern Texas; it is eaten by some Native Americans to, among other things, experience a vision.) Developments during the nineteenth century have been characterized by the Christianization of some religious activities, the spread of Peyotism, and the adoption of new "cults"—but also the reinvigoration of religious tribalism.

The contribution of Sheepeater religion to Shoshoni religion represents a separate issue and the extent of its influence is difficult to judge. There is some evidence that the concepts of mountain spirits and rock ogres were particularly characteristic of this religion.[12] On the other hand, the interaction among the various groups of the Wind River Shoshoni so thoroughly blended the several kinds of religious influence that today it is not possible to separate the different strands.

The following presentation of Shoshoni religion is an interpretation of the forms practiced by medicine men and women and traditionalists until very recent times. Today, practically all of the old-style medicine men and women are gone, and those who now claim to be a medicine man or woman operate without the benefit of the complete traditional setting, combining glimpses of Shoshoni practice with a pan-Indian outlook. If we want to study the earlier style of Wind River Shoshoni religion as once practiced during their days as a hunting people, we have to rely on the testimony given by traditional Shoshoni believers, who preserve many of the beliefs and practices of an age long past.

The Structure of Shoshoni Religion: Spirits, Powers and Supernatural Power, and Visions

Supreme Being: Mythology of Wolf and "Our Father" in Everyday Religion

The complex historical background of Shoshoni culture and religion is reflected in the composite character of Wind River Shoshoni religion as known in recent times. This is conspicuous especially in the remarkable gap between everyday religious practice and mythology. The mythology expresses the ancient world of the hunters and gatherers of the Great Basin, depicting the landscape, the life-style, and the animal figures of the Great Basin Shoshoni. The stories themselves are common to the Numic tribes of that area and the Wind River Shoshoni east of the Rocky Mountains. On the other hand, the religion practiced in everyday life presents a sharp contrast, referring to a world and life-style predominantly Plains Indian in character. Most of the active spirits in everyday religion, too, are animal figures, but these are animals found on the Plains. For example, the buffalo spirit has no importance in the mythic tales, but it turns up again and again in vision narratives and historical legends and plays an important role in rituals. Also the rituals of everyday religion are very similar to those of Plains Indians—the Sun Dance is a good example.

The gap between mythology and everyday religion creates a tension in Shoshoni religion, a tension that sometimes leads to openly conflicting views on the same subject. Take for instance the belief in a Supreme Being. Some scholars have thought that this belief is fairly recent, an outcome of Christian missionary teaching, and that in earlier Shoshoni religion there was only belief in many spirits all on the same level. However, there is plenty of evidence that not only the Wyoming Shoshoni but also the Shoshoneans of the Great Basin have believed in a Supreme Being since ancient times. This divinity is almost everywhere called "father." He is sometimes thought of as anthropomorphic, that is, humanlike, and sometimes as zoomorphic, or animallike; in the latter case he is portrayed as **Wolf,** a wolf that speaks with a human tongue and thinks human thoughts.

Among the Wind River Shoshoni he is Wolf in mythology, but not in everyday religion. The mythology tells us that he supervises the world, an Indian chief in the disguise of a wolf, aided by "little wolf," or Coyote, a trickster who pulls many pranks. His surrounding host of figures are all represented as animals, although (as in the Greek fables) their thinking and actions are predominantly human. At the end of the ancient mythological times all these zoomorphic beings turned into real animals and became the ancestors of now living animal species. In the mythological world Wolf is not so much the creator as the arranger of an already existing world. Coyote is partly his assistant in this work, partly his adversary, blamed for having introduced death into the world. Mostly, however, Coyote is just a trickster with bad habits.

In everyday religion the scene is different. In the first place, the mythological dualism is gone. Coyote plays no role at all, and no cult is directed to him. The primordial animal characters of mythology—Porcupine, Skunk, Weasel, Cottontail, and so on—have given way to other animal spirits that appear in visions. Most important, Wolf has disappeared, and in his place a vaguely anthropomorphic Supreme Being, "Our Father" (**Tam Apo**), has made his entrance. He is, at least in later tradition, supposed to be the creator of the world and of humans and may be manifested in the sun. In the old days, people told me, there was not much worship of Our Father. Only in exceptional cases—for instance when a person was all alone out on the plains suffering from thirst, hunger, or cold—did he or she turn in prayer to the Supreme Being as a last resort. Usually they prayed to auxiliary spirits. However, from about 1800 when the Sun Dance was introduced, people could more easily approach their high god in the annual ceremonies. In this way the godhead became more active. At least in one medicine man's theology a kind of hierarchical structure developed, with "Our Father" being enthroned above the mass of spirits whom he controls and directs.

One of my informants, now dead, gave me the following description of *Tam Apo* and of the cult associated with him:

We think about him as the whole sky; he covers the whole world. He is a human being above the sky. His power extends over the whole earth. In ancient times we did not pray to him, but we prayed to different spirits. Still, we believed in God. Only in the Sun Dance did we pray directly to God.

However, this is not the general situation of Shoshoni beliefs. For most traditional Shoshoni, the spirits work largely independent of the Supreme Being. When people need individual help they turn to their guardian spirits or to medicine men and women whose possession of such spirits enables them to help people out. When aid is sought for the whole tribe or for individuals coming together, they call on Our Father, especially in the Sun Dance. The nature of the Supreme Being in recent times can be seen in the following prayer to *Tam Apo* at the sunrise ceremony by a leader of the Sun Dance in 1948:

> *Tam Apo,* here we are, standing up and facing towards the sunrise. I am offering a prayer again, asking your blessing. The sun you made has come up, it is shining towards us, all over; and it is the light from you and we like to have this every day of our life, and we want to live a long time. Because we are suffering for our homes, families, friends, and all kinds of nations, I want you to bless us. And I ask you to bless the service boys [in the U.S. Armed Forces] so that they will be safe and nothing will happen to them. . . . I ask you to see to it that there will be no war, make it that way through your willpower. And when we get to the end of these three days, when we get out, give us our water and our food. The powerful water will give us good strength, and so will the food—what we eat will give us good strength. For we want to live as long as we possibly can.

How can we account for this discrepancy of beliefs in a Supreme Being—on the one hand mythological tales focusing on Wolf and on the other hand ritual practices directed to "Our Father" (*Tam Apo*)? Because of the divergence in beliefs in a Supreme Being, it may appear that the whole tribe suffers from a split personality, but this is not the case. Rather, this discrepancy is the direct influence of two distinct religious traditions having their roots in different cultural milieus upon the Shoshoni religious heritage. Of course, for some Shoshoni Indians the old stories of Wolf and Coyote are just "fictional" tales not to be taken seriously (something like Grimm's fairy tales for modern Europeans and Americans). These tales are usually told during the dark seasons of the year (as with most American Indian storytelling) as entertainment both for grownups and children, but mostly for children. Some stories about the Cannibal Owl and other monsters that are supposed to catch and devour children are more than anything else pedagogical tales told to make children behave properly.

However, in the Great Basin area this mythology has been a matter of belief, and among the Wind River Shoshoni such mythological tales are considered to be "true stories." For example, stories such as the myth of how Coyote brought death into the world are not "fictional" tales but a subject of belief—at least, that was the case during my field research some thirty years ago. Therefore, the discrepancy of beliefs in a Supreme Being in mythology and everyday religion cannot be dismissed as the difference between religion and "fictional" accounts (or fairy tales). The best way to understand the relationship between the two kinds of belief is to observe how the individual deals personally with the tension and to see how different social settings call into play different orientations of religious beliefs. Viewing Shoshoni religion in this fashion enables us to understand how it is possible for an individual to isolate particular sets of belief for particular situations. For example, when Shoshoni Indians spend a winter evening listening to mythological stories they may accept the mythological figures and believe in their world and activities; the reactions of the listeners around the storyteller may vary from credulity to amusement to skepticism. By contrast, in another setting, the summer Sun Dance celebration, all religious belief is concentrated on the anthropomorphic Supreme Being and the spirits surrounding him. And as we shall see later, in a third situation, when an individual dreams of guardian spirits, the Supreme Being does not appear at all. This demonstrates that in the hunting religion of the Shoshoni beliefs are not codified in a neat system such as a formal theology (as found in Christianity and Islam). Rather, the individual experiences the supernatural world in what could be called alternating configurations or compartments. Different religious complexes appear in different cultural and social situations. There are even watertight compartments separating these religious complexes, so that the mythteller can speak about a Supreme Being in animal form, while the Sun Dance dancer refers to a Supreme Being in human form. The tensions among various aspects of Shoshoni religion show us the flexible nature of Native American religion and also throw light on the composite character of all religious traditions.[13]

Spirits and Powers

Everyday religious life, sometimes called "practical religion," is quite different from the beliefs and tales of mythology. In everyday religion the Supreme Being is always thought to reside in the sky and may express his splendor through the sun, but the stars do not play any role in religious ritual. (Conversely, the stars and constellations figure frequently in the mythological tales, where they are transformations of the mythological beings.) However, next to the Supreme Being there is a class of spirits of the atmosphere that are powerful, although they are not greater than the Supreme Being. There are many of these spirits or powers in the atmosphere and throughout nature, some more important than others, but they are not arranged in a clear hierarchy or "theology."

One particular atmospheric power is inherent in the first thunder to be heard in the spring. Prayers to the thunder spirits at this time promote health and well-being. Lightning spirits and thunder spirits are sometimes identified with each other, sometimes conceived of as independent of each other. An old Shoshoni woman informed me that small brown birds that jump up and down close to the creeks— apparently blackbirds—control the thunder. The lightning, on the other hand, she ascribed to the activities of a bird with a red spot that she had seen at Trout Creek. She was here obviously referring to the hummingbird.

An aged medicine man had somewhat different ideas, although he shared the old woman's opinion that the thunderbird has a diminutive form. To him, **tongwoyaget** ("crying clouds") is like a hummingbird, but even smaller. He seems like "a sharp-nosed bird, little as a thumb, looks like the hummingbird, but is faster." This is how the thunderbird looked in his visionary dreams. The same informant was convinced that the thunderbird collects the water in the clouds and makes them thunder. This gives us rain and snow, he said. Lightning he had seen as a fire or as a blue streak of light, but never as a being. It can talk to people in his dreams, however. In practice, however, this medicine man could not separate distinctly between thunder and lightning spirits.

The idea that the thunder spirit looks like a hummingbird is apparently an old one among Indians of the Uto-Aztecan linguistic stock to whom the Shoshoni belong, for the ancient protective god of the Aztecs, Huitzilopochtli, was connected with hummingbirds. Actually, his name means "hummingbird to the left," and two hummingbirds decorated his statue in the great temple of Tenochtitlán, present-day Mexico City.

There is also, however, the notion among the Shoshoni that the thunderbird looks like an eagle. This is a general Plains idea the Shoshoni have possibly taken over from other Plains tribes. The eagle itself is respected by the Shoshoni as the bird of peace, connected with the sky and the Supreme Being. As a messenger from God a stuffed eagle is placed in its nest on the top of the Sun Dance pole.

Other atmospheric spirits are the winds. While some winds are controlled by the thunderbirds, others are subordinated to **nyipij,** the "wind master." Nobody has seen this spirit, whose appearance is unknown, but Indians sense its presence; its residence is high in the mountains. Whirlwinds are apparitions of dead people and may be dangerous, as illustrated in the following account. Not long ago a company of women were out walking. They encountered a whirlwind. One of the women got angry and cursed the whirlwind. It turned against her, destroyed her tent, and broke one of her legs.

Atmospheric spirits are numerous; there are also many other spirits closer to the human landscape, spirits associated with animals, plants, mountains, and lakes. The spirits assume various forms, as can be expected in a religion dominated by visions, and they exercise different powers—some benevolent, some malevolent. These spirits are so numerous we can only touch on a few here.

One of the most respected of all spirits is **tam sogobia,** "Our Mother Earth." The Supreme Being and the powers associated with him, especially Mother Earth, completely dominate the Sun Dance. Mother Earth receives offerings in the Sun Dance (tobacco is poured on the surface of the earth) and appears in ever so many prayers. Whenever there is a feast and the bowl of water is brought in, a little water is first poured on the ground for Mother Earth. She is identical with the earth itself and nourishes the plants and animals on which human beings live.

The spirits that dwell close to humans may be met in the surrounding natural environment and in visionary and dream experiences. We do not find, however, that spirits occupy houses or ranches. The idea of house spirits does not belong to a hunting people who not long ago lived in *tipis* transported from place to place. The spirits are found in nature. The locations of spirits are places avoided by humans, because they are sacred and dangerous places. The boundary line between these two categories is vague, but the common element is that they are risky for people to visit.

Sacred and dangerous places do occur all over the land that the Wind River Shoshoni once roamed, from Salt Lake City to the Medicine Bow Mountains and Yellowstone Park. Our comments will be restricted to the lands that the Shoshoni have occupied during the past hundred years, the Wind River Valley and Wind River Mountains, and to the areas they frequent in the Grand Teton and Yellowstone parks. Because the Shoshoni have inhabited this area since ancient times (and were not moved to a reservation distant from their ancient homelands, as with some tribes), the sacred places within this general area are very old.

The sagebrush plains have few sacred places, except among rivers and creeks and in the high scraggy hills. The verdure of the Wind River and its confluences has been the hiding place of the feared dwarf spirits called **nynymbi,** which are usually unseen but sometimes may be dressed in old-fashioned buckskin suits and armed with bows and arrows. These dwarf spirits are evil. They shoot arrows into the lone traveler so that the latter falls from his or her horse with a hemorrhage in the lungs. This is a supernatural explanation for the many cases of tuberculosis among the Shoshoni. The *nynymbi* may also be found in the mountains, and there are many legends of these spirits being attacked by eagles. If a Shoshoni shoots an eagle, the dwarf spirit shows thankfulness by helping the person find a dead game animal. (This story is a version of the widespread Indian tale of the battle between the heavenly eagles and the dark powers of the earth and the underworld.)

In the waters there are water sprites of various kinds, such as water babies, the water woman (usually just one), and water buffalo. Formerly, water babies could be heard crying in the Wind River.

They sound like babies and look like small human beings. They are one and a half feet tall but so heavy that one cannot move them. One of them may devour a woman's baby and put itself in the baby's place. The water woman, or fish woman, with pretty, long hair is a full-sized water spirit. She is counted as a kind of water baby and is supposed to be evil, dragging people down through a hole in the ice. Some skeptic Shoshoni suggest that white trappers introduced this belief. This is possible, for in several tales she has a long fish tail like a European sea maiden. Nevertheless, she has been seen by Shoshoni Indians in the Big Wind River, Bull Lake, and the Dinwoody Lakes.

Bull Lake is a favorite haunt of water sprites. In particular it houses the remarkable water buffalo. (In Shoshoni Bull Lake is called "water buffalo lake.") They look like buffalo but are supernatural. They can be heard in the spring when the ice cracks. There is a story of how two Shoshoni scouts found a water buffalo on the shore and killed it. One of the men ate pieces of the buffalo. His comrade watched him gradually turn into a buffalo, go down into the water, and disappear. Bull Lake is a dangerous place; many Shoshoni stayed away from it in the old days. They were respectful when passing the lake and abstained from making fun of it. If a person happened to see a water buffalo there, it was a bad sign.

The buttes and foothills are full of spirits. On the north side of Crowheart Butte, a legendary place in Shoshoni war records, there are said to be lots of spirits that may be good guardian spirits if you receive their help. However, it is dangerous to climb the butte, for the person who does so may disappear. Other buttes are sites of rock drawings, and the spirits are in their neighborhood. Thus, there are several reports of people receiving a guardian spirit in a vision at Medicine Butte and Cedar Buttes and in the foothills at the headwaters of Sage Creek, Willow Creek, and Owl Creek. The rock drawings are supposed to represent spirits and have been made in the winter by these spirits themselves. Each spirit draws its picture. Indians have told me that in the spring and summer they have discovered new drawings on the rockface, apparently pecked by spirits since their last visit. Some Shoshoni who approach the rock drawing places in wintertime may hear the spirits working at them. As they come closer, the sound ceases. When they withdraw from the place they can again hear the knocking.

The spirits are not as common today as they were in the old days. The power lines and poles especially have scared them away. They have retreated for good to the mountains. Even rock drawing sites have been abandoned. When a white built a cabin close to the rock drawings at Sage Creek, Indian vision seekers did not go there anymore—it was useless.

At South Fork Canyon (of Little Wind River) there is a deep cave where until about 1910 the Shoshoni buried their dead. The corpses were carried on horses up the steep slopes and laid side by side. The place is avoided.

The high mountains were formerly haunted by dangerous spirits, the **dzoavits** or **pandzoavits**. They were humanlike monsters made of stone with stone packs on their backs; but their faces and hands were of soft material. They ate people and could come to the camps to do so. It was risky to talk about them. Most Shoshoni I asked said that this kind of spirit is extinct nowadays. However, they may exist underground and underwater.

The majestic Teton peaks are powerful beings. They do not allow people to climb them, and those who try succumb. Nor do they accept being called by their right name, which in Shoshoni is "black standing up." If a person traveling through the Teton Pass makes use of their true name, it will cause a flood or, in wintertime, a terrible snowstorm. It is also forbidden to point at the peaks with a finger. Like other northwestern Plains Indians, the Shoshoni once feared the geyser basins of Yellowstone Park, ascribing their activi-

Spiritual power radiates like electricity from pandzoavits *(depicted here in a rock drawing), the dangerous, mysterious ogre and visionary spirit of the Shoshoni.*

ties to dangerous spirits. However, in this respect the Sheepeaters were less fearful, having made the park their home.[14]

There is a medicine wheel close to Pinedale, west of the Wind River Mountains. Some Shoshoni Indians say it is a plan of the sacred Sun Dance, its spokes corresponding to the "rays" left by the dancers on the sandy ground of the Sun Dance hall. In modern times at least one Shoshoni has gone up there to sleep between the spokes to receive a power dream. Not far away from this place is a rock in the mountains around which Indians have to pass to be safe when traveling. However, people dare not walk there unless they bring a gift; to go without making an offering is to invite bad luck.

The examples of sacred places given here could be complemented with others farther away from the Wind River Reservation, but still situated in ancient Shoshoni country. They all give evidence that there are sacred places scattered around the territory used by the Shoshoni, so that a wanderer or mounted traveler always has to be prepared for ritual precautions. Indeed, one may never know for sure when one might be confronted by a supernatural being, for it belongs to the essence of these spirits that they can reveal themselves anywhere and at any time. This is the case in particular with all those spirits that may provide an individual with **puha**, supernatural power. These are the guardian spirits and are also called *puha*.

Puha: Supernatural Power, Visions, and Guardian Spirits

With the mention of guardian spirit beliefs we enter the central tenets of old Shoshoni religion. All the previously mentioned spirits of the atmosphere and nature, including "Our Father" and Mother Earth, possess a kind of power. However, Shoshoni distinguish the power of spirits in general from *puha*, which can mean either supernatural power acquired by humans or guardian spirits who grant such supernatural power. *Puha* is central to Shoshoni religion because the heart of this tradition is receiving supernatural power from guardian spirits, especially through visions and dreams.

The persons who have power from the spirits are not so numerous today as in former times, when all males were supposed to withdraw into the solitude of the wilderness to obtain the favors of the spirits. Still, there are some Shoshoni today who have such powers, although they do not like to talk about it. Nowadays *puha* is received in spontaneous dreams or in dreams during unconscious states due to exhaustion in Sun Dance dancing. Earlier, persons interested in supernatural power submitted themselves to the strains of a vision quest to get it.

In Shoshoni tradition, dreams and the vision quest have long been acceptable means of receiving power, but the acquisition of supernatural power in spontaneous dreams is probably the older way, with roots in Great Basin culture. The vision quest probably came later, institutionalized through the influence from the Plains Indians. Thereafter, the two ways existed side by side until, after the Indian wars and the establishment of the reservation system, it was found to be rather superfluous to seek visions for warfare, prowess, and hunting in a time that no longer had use of such pursuits. During World War I, a medicine man received a vision according to which all deliberately sought visions were imparted by *pandzoavits* and therefore dangerous to the visionary. This message was in a way a rationalization of the gradual disappearance of the vision quest. It also signaled the return of the importance of spontaneous dreams.

In view of the modern revival of vision quests among such Plains peoples as the Cheyenne and the Lakota, it is possible that the vision quest has regained some of its old status among some Shoshoni who still cling to traditional beliefs. However, during my first visit to the Shoshoni in 1948 there were only a few persons, among them the famous medicine man Tudy Roberts, who were supposed to have power from sought visions. (The career of Tudy Roberts will be presented later.) Another medicine man offered to go through a vision quest together with me, an offer that was not realized because of the onset of cold weather (the appropriate time for vision quests, the summer, was over).

Stories of people who have experienced the vision quest circulate among Shoshoni, but they all refer to persons who are now dead. Although the Shoshoni have been more open and direct about their religious beliefs and experiences than most Plains Indians, they do not volunteer to disclose the details of their visionary experiences except to close kin and friends. However, the main elements of their experiences are known and even told to non-Indians.

The general rules of the Shoshoni vision quest have been the following. The supplicant, usually male, rides a horse up to the foothills where the rock drawings are—the latter are the foremost places of spirit revelation. At a distance of some 200 yards from the rock with pictographs he tethers his horse. Then he takes a bath to cleanse himself in the nearest creek or lake. Without moccasins he walks up to the rock ledge just beneath the drawings and makes his camp there. Naked except for a blanket around him, he lies down there under the open sky, waiting for the spirits to appear. Sometimes, I was told, the supplicant directs a prayer to a particular spirit depicted on the rock panel, anxious to receive that very spirit's power. As we shall see, each spirit that blesses its client does so with a special gift related to the spirit's own abilities.

The vision is induced by fasting, enduring the cold and lack of sleep, and smoking the pipe. Sometimes the vision comes rather quickly, in other cases after a longer time, and in still other cases not at all. There are reports that the vision appears after three or four nights and days, but this information may be doubtful, constructed perhaps to make the nights of suffering conform with the sacred numbers three or four.

It is difficult to tell whether the Indian is awake or dreaming when he finally is blessed with a vision. The Shoshoni word **navu-shieip** covers both states. One medicine man told me that he had spontaneously received waking visions, and they appeared like dreams. He also made a distinction between common dreams and "power dreams," that is, dreams or visions in which spirits turn up. These dreams are, he said, more clear than other dreams and hold your attention so you cannot awake until they are over. There is also a peculiar feeling that you are going away somewhere.[15]

What appears in the vision itself may be quite changeable. The same medicine man said that he had had a vision of a lightning spirit that changed its shape: it was first like a body of water, then like a human being, then like an animal, and finally it faded away. We shall soon see more examples of this spiritual ability. It is obvious that the spirit of the dream or vision takes part of the latter's inconstancy and changing panorama. Some instances of sought visions among Shoshoni may give further illustrations of the drama and visual contents involved.

Taivotsi ("Little White Man") had a dream in which he was informed in a mysterious way that he should go to the rock drawings of Willow Creek if he wanted to get medicine. He did as he was told. He cleansed himself from impurity by bathing there, and early in the evening he lay down. He did not quite know if he was asleep or not, but thought he was awake when an owl suddenly flew down upon him and started pecking him. The owl tried to scare him away but did not succeed and finally left him. A little later there appeared a bear. It grabbed hold of Taivotsi and threw him around. Taivotsi, however, did not care, so the bear gave up and trotted off. Next, a deer came forth and jumped straight at Taivotsi. It repeated this movement several times, but Taivotsi remained calm. A coyote then stole upon him and bit him, but Taivotsi did not mind. Finally, a big rattlesnake came writhing against him, rattling its tail. Taivotsi had always been afraid of snakes, so he jumped up and ran away. That was his misfortune. If he had stayed on the spot, the snake would have entrusted him with supernatural medicine, for this snake was the spirit. Instead, his legs became lame shortly afterward, and he was forced to walk with crutches.

This story demonstrates what deprivations the supplicant has to experience, and what psychic strength he must possess. Four visitations strike him that he has to endure. Finally, there comes the spirit itself. When the client flees from it he has not only forfeited his luck, he has also committed a crime against the spirit, a crime punished by paralysis. Many a vision seeker does not even come that far. If there are no trials from dangerous animals, this is a sign that the spirit does not accept him as its ward. It may be that the spirit does not consider him humble and good-natured or that he has not made the right ritual preparations. Of course, a supplicant who cannot face the four fearsome animals (four being the sacred number) has no chance to meet the spirit.

The appearance of the spirit is the great moment in the vision quest. Sometimes the seeker is not aware that he stands before the spirit itself, as in Taivotsi's case. Usually, however, there is no doubt. "The *puha* approaches you like a strong light," said one Shoshoni medicine man. The mysterious way of spirits is well accounted for in Morgan Moon's memories of his visionary experiences. Once, when he was lying in trance, a spirit looking like an Indian slowly approached him. It stopped at his feet, granted him its supernatural medicine, and sang for him its sacred song. Then, as it were, the spirit dissolved, gradually fading away. In vain Morgan tried to find it. On another occasion Morgan saw the spirit emerge from the willow thicket and slowly approach him. It handed over to him its powers and the instructions connected with the power. Then it turned around and went back into the willow brush. In an instant it was gone.

Mysterious appearance, transference of power, imparting instructions with the power (such as rules for dress and the wearing of feathers, rules for making a medicine bundle, or rules for avoiding things, persons, or actions), singing of a sacred song—these are the guardian spirit's activities in a successful vision quest. It is then the client's task to take on the responsibility for the right administration of the marvelous gifts. Careless manipulation of the power, disobedience of the rules laid down, and neglect of ritual observances leads implacably to loss of power, paralysis, or other disease, injury, or even death.

However, in some cases where the **"medicine"** has been lost, the spirit may again take pity on its former ward. Let us return to Taivotsi. In one vision quest he met a falcon spirit that endowed him with the ability to win in the so-called handgame, one of the most popular pastimes among the Plains Indians. There were certain conditions for the reception of this gift, and Taivotsi unfortunately happened to transgress them. As a consequence he became almost blind. Sometime afterward he was walking over the plains when suddenly the same spirit again showed itself to him. "You trespassed against my instructions," the spirit said. "Now you are a poor fellow. However, I feel pity on you. I will help you once again. Tomorrow you shall go to Willow Creek. You will find a huge deer there. This deer you shall have." Next morning Taivotsi rode to the place that the spirit had pointed out to him. His sight was bad, and he did not indulge in great expectations. But lo, there was a big deer! He killed it and returned home with it. Thereafter his sight changed and became as sharp as it had been in the good old days. And the spirit often appeared to him and told him where to hunt with success.

These vision narratives tell us that the guardian spirit may show itself as a person or as an animal. From the material at my disposal it seems that the animal form is more common. At least one medicine man who had many guardian spirits referred to animal shapes in 95 percent of the cases. As stated before, this is natural in a hunting religion. As we have noticed, the change from animal to human being and vice versa is the usual thing in these visions. The animal form says possibly something about the nature of the power that the visionary receives. The beaver makes the person a good swimmer, the deer or antelope a swift runner, the magpie a good scout, and so on: each of these special abilities relates to the abilities of the animal form of the protective spirit. There are certain conditions on the use of this power. For instance, the deer spirit whose gift is quick running may direct its client to have a deer tail fixed to his shirt or hanging on a ribbon around his neck. The client may also be told to pray to the spirit about power before, say, a running competition.

Possessors of Power: Medicine Men, Visionaries, and Shamans

Shoshoni visionaries could acquire several guardian spirits one after another, sometimes in such a way that one spirit paved the way for the other. One medicine man even constructed a hierarchy of spirits, with the lightning spirit on top and with other spirits of lesser dignity subordinated in a descending scale. This was, however, not a typical case. The guardian spirit world is rather chaotic to most Shoshoni as the spirits operate as they please.

The medicine man, or inspired healer, has the largest number of spirits and is an expert on spirit lore. Otherwise he is little distinguished from other visionaries, except that he is usually blessed by spirits that have given him the ability to cure sick people. Such spirits are often stronger than other spirits. This was the case particularly in the past when medicine men could travel in their spirits to the land of the dead to receive information or liberate some lost soul that had been taken there by the dead. However, a spirit that gives curing *puha* may also give other abilities that have nothing at all to do with curing.

The medicine men have always been few in Shoshoni society. It is indeed difficult to know their numbers even in comparatively recent times, for two reasons. First, there is no proper term for a "medicine man"—both common visionaries and medicine men are called **pu-hagan**, or "possessors of power." This linguistic usage reflects the only slight difference between a medicine man and an ordinary Shoshoni, at least in older times when most men were supposed to seek out guardian spirits. Second, there have been many individuals with supernatural power who have been able to handle minor diseases without being considered medicine men. A real medicine man cures many difficult diseases (with some exceptions given below) and is socially accepted as a doctor. During my stay among the Shoshoni only five persons passed as medicine men, but several other persons were supposed to have power to heal a few minor, narrowly defined diseases. This should be compared with the estimation of some Shoshoni that in the old days about 10 percent of the population were *puhagan*. Perhaps a tenth of these *puhagan* were proper medicine men.

Some women may become medicine women. However, this happens late in life. As long as they are young and menstruate, they are impure and cannot approach the spirits. Only after menopause can they establish a connection with the spirits. This means that there are no particular spirits for women, as there are in other hunting cultures; not even Mother Earth is accessible to young women. It also means that they cannot, like young men, participate in vision quests. However, older women after menopause are free to pursue vision quests, unless they receive their power in dreams. Some medicine women have been very powerful. One such woman, the mother of one of my informants, a medicine man, was reputed to have healed a sick person just by touching him once with her hand. During my time among the Shoshoni I met two medicine women, both very capable.

Some medicine men are specialized in curing rattlesnake bites, or pneumonia, or other specific diseases. A clever medicine man is also expected to show his spiritual abilities in ways other than curing. He may be able to disclose the whereabouts of the game animals, to find lost items, or to foretell the future. Such competent medicine men who have recourse to some sort of trance are known to us as shamans.

One particular kind of medicine man that used to exist among the Shoshoni and Paiute of the Great Basin were the antelope medicine men. They had supernatural power to attract the antelope (pronghorns). Together with his tribesmen such a medicine man would go out to the antelope flats carrying a gourd decorated with antelope hooves. Standing on a hilltop, he shook the gourd and sang the "antelope song." This song called the animals and ended with a sound imitating them. The antelope drew near and were surrounded by the hunters, who easily caught or killed them. There are no antelope medicine men left today.

Strictly speaking, these antelope medicine men are not doctors, and therefore not medicine men in our sense of the word. However, the Shoshoni consider them medicine men because of their great powers and perhaps also because they serve the whole community. As we have seen, "medicine man" is a white concept. To the Shoshoni, "a *puhagan* with great *puha*" is a more adequate expression, implying that the great *puha* may be used for the help of others, whether for curing or for a collective antelope hunt. One medicine man went so far as designating himself and his colleagues "sacred" because of their possession of *puha*. However, there has been no particular veneration of medicine men, but rather great fear of them if they were known for turning their powers against people. Such medicine men appeared in the past and were shunned because they practiced witchcraft. All medicine men who use their powers for the good of the tribe are respected in proportion to their ability.

Medicine men are usually forceful personalities who, because of their knowledge of the supernatural, are valuable as ceremonial leaders, for instance in the Sun Dance. All Shoshoni ceremonies are based on some revelatory experiences with which medicine men are quite familiar. It is therefore natural that they sponsor a Sun Dance, or lead such a dance, or perform curing rites in the ceremonial hall of the dance. We shall later see how the medicine men proceed when they cure their patients.

Death and the Land of the Dead

When the medicine man's art fails, as it finally does, his patient leaves for the world of the dead. For the Shoshoni, there are many ways of conceiving of the dead. Either they go to a particular realm in the other world, or they remain on earth as ghosts, or they are born again as people, or they transmigrate into insects, birds, or even inanimate objects like wood and rocks. There is also the belief, possibly post-Christian, that the dead person goes to Our Father. The beliefs in reincarnation and transmigration seem to have been very weak and to have disappeared at least fifty years ago. All these afterlife alternatives illustrate what we have said above about so-called alternating configurations of belief: they are adapted to particular situations and are called into focus when such situations come up.

The beliefs in a land of the dead are not really vital today but deserve being mentioned. Medicine men who have gone there in trance, and sick people who have been there in coma, tell about this land. One Shoshoni woman, the granddaughter of Chief Washakie, "died"—which in their language also means lost consciousness—and found herself in a foreign place looking down from a high hill. She saw the land of the dead, a pretty country with many *tipis* and people. Other "travelers" report the same thing, adding a detail or two here and there: you arrive in that land through a tunnel; the dead sleep in the day, but are up in the night; they spend the time there singing, dancing, and gambling; they hunt buffalo on horseback in beautiful surroundings. In short, this is the blessed land of the dead of the Plains Indians. We have reasons to suspect that in the pre-horse, pre-Plains days the Shoshoni land of the dead had a slightly different tone, being more in line with the concept of the afterlife held by the Great Basin tribes. However, even in earlier times this land was described as delightful and happy with plenty of food.

To come to this paradise the dead person follows the Milky Way, "the backbone of the world." This indicates a realm of the dead in heaven, an old belief also found among the Basin Shoshoni. This belief is somewhat at variance with another belief in which the land of the dead is situated beyond the mountains.

There is a very strong belief in ghosts that haunt the living. Some say that these ghosts are the dead who have followed the wrong branch of the Milky Way and turned back. The idea seems to be that good tribal people go to the land beyond, while those who have behaved badly (for instance, killed or robbed a member of the tribe) come back to wander eternally "as a man, as a voice, as an echo" (as one Shoshoni expressed it). Ghosts might disguise themselves as whirlwinds. Some ghosts appear as walking skeletons; they are visible in the moonlight and frighten people with their rattling. Favors done for these ghosts may result in their granting supernatural powers to their benefactors—however, this is rare. Usually ghosts afflict people in some way, and even medicine men may be hurt by contact with them.

Personal experiences and legends elaborate the ideas of the afterlife. However, most Shoshoni express only a slight interest in the next life and often declare that they know nothing about it—the dead do not come back to tell us. Only those who themselves in trance or coma have gone to the other world are more explicit about what it is like. Here, as elsewhere among the Shoshoni, the rule holds that only visions and dreams open the gates of the other world.

Structure Summary: Honoring Spirits and Acquiring Power

Shoshoni religion is as complex as the total Shoshoni cultural heritage, with roots in the Great Basin traditions and more recent contributions from Plains traditions. As was seen with basic beliefs about the Supreme Being, the Shoshoni have both mythological notions of Wolf and ritual practices directed to "Our Father." Shoshoni religion may be seen as a composite of various strands within different Shoshoni groups and influence from the major Plains traditions; but, as we saw in Chapter I, every religious tradition, even a world religion, is the sum total of its previous history and therefore is a kind of composite religion. Shoshoni religion, like every religious tradition, incorporates various historical influences while forming a distinctive worldview. The several religious complexes present within the Shoshoni tradition are experienced by the individual as a whole worldview.

The hunting culture and religious tradition of Shoshoni are more loosely organized even than life among horticulturalists, for example, the Zuni (to be discussed in the next chapter). There is no codified "theology," and yet the Shoshoni worldview presents a clear and consistent picture of religious reality. Central to this worldview is the reality of spirits, some of which are important in the mythological tales forming a distinctive religious complex of beliefs and stories; other spirits are related to the separate religious complex of everyday ritual life. Paramount among these spirits is Our Father, who is located in the sky, associated with the sun, and worshiped in the all-important Sun Dance. In addition to Our Father, there are many atmospheric spirits such as thunder, lightning, and wind (and associated birds). These atmospheric forces have power, which is dangerous, and may even be used to harm humans, as in the case of the whirlwind. Other forces of what in English is called "nature" are also spirits. Not all of nature is sacred for the Shoshoni, but certain natural phenomena such as mountains and lakes are viewed as having special association with certain spirits. Mother Earth is one of the most important of these spirits, to whom offerings are made in the Sun Dance and on many other religious occasions. As we will see in the next section, the erection of the Sun Dance lodge during the Sun Dance ceremony is a ritual reconstruction of the world, a microcosm. Places where spirits are found are sacred, and some locations are so powerful or so filled with evil spirits that it is dangerous for people to visit them: sacred and dangerous places are approached with caution or avoided. Some specific places are especially sacred or dangerous, but generally the nomadic heritage of the Shoshoni has meant that these places are scattered throughout the territory they roamed; there is no special sacredness to the home or a permanent dwelling place such as a village. In Shoshoni tradition, supernatural beings may reveal themselves at any place or time, and the individual must always be ready to recognize and revere them. Generally a Shoshoni should live life in harmony with these spirits, respecting and praying to them, honoring sacred places and avoiding dangerous places. There are special rules such as not saying the true name of the Teton peaks or pointing a finger at them. Honoring the spirits and sacred places enhances one's life; neglecting the spirits and overstepping the bounds of dangerous places invites misfortune.

These spirits and sacred places are important, but the heart of Shoshoni religion is the *puha* or supernatural power of guardian spirits, which individuals can receive through a sought vision or a dream. As has been mentioned throughout, the flexibility of Shoshoni religion is mainly due to the Shoshoni emphasis on changing beliefs and rituals in line with newly received visions or dreams of supernatural power. In earlier times every young man was expected to seek a vision and receive a guardian spirit, undergoing lengthy and arduous ritual procedures; in recent times the dream has become more important as a means of obtaining supernatural power. The important Shoshoni religious leaders are the "possessors of power," the medicine men, visionaries, and shamans who have received supernatural power, usually only after the difficult ordeal of the vision quest or the Sun Dance. These are the religious figures with the power to heal, to take the lead in important ceremonies such as the Sun Dance, and to initiate the hunt. The gist of Shoshoni religion is to maintain purity and honor spirits and sacred places, while seeking the supernatural power of visions and dreams. It should be noted that although much of this questing for supernatu-

ral power is individual, it usually benefits the community as a
whole, as seen in the collective blessing in the Sun Dance or in the
antelope medicine man's aid in the collective hunt.

The Dynamics of Shoshoni Religion: Rituals of Human Change, the Sun Dance, and Curing

The many ideas and notions of the supernatural are not just philosophical concepts to the Shoshoni, thought tools to explain the
world around them, although of course they also fulfill this intellec-
tual ambition. They are lived through, experienced, "danced out,"
as the great European scholar R. R. Marett expressed it at the beginning of this century. Notions of the supernatural are inextricably associated with daily life, with rites, and with observances.

Here we must nevertheless be careful not to draw hasty conclu-
sions: the *beliefs* are transformed into active ritual behavior, but the
myths are not. We saw how mythology operates at variance with
religious beliefs, sometimes even contradicting them. Mythology
represents an older worldview and thus does not reflect everyday religious reality, with a few exceptions. A ritual like the Sun Dance,
for example, has a foundation legend—that is, a story of the meeting between supernaturals and mortals in what is described as historical times. There is no foundation myth, however—that is, a tale
of divine decisions in distant mythic times. The Sun Dance is a creation of Plains religions and has nothing to do with the mythology
developed while the Shoshoni were part of the Great Basin cultural
area.

In this connection we should observe that the Shoshoni rituals are
relatively few in comparison to those of, for instance, the Zuni. As a
hunting people they concentrated on the rituals of human change,
of curing, and of thanksgiving. Of these, the original thanksgiving
rite has given way to the Plains Indian Sun Dance, which is indeed a
ceremony with the same aims, but it is much more intricate.

We may well wonder what has become of animal ceremonialism,
so typical for hunting peoples in the northern area of the continent.
The answer is that it does exist among the Shoshoni, but rather rudi-
mentarily. In mythology there are numerous references to the resuscitation of game animals from their preserved bones; sometimes the

requirement is that the bones be thrown into water. There is also the story of a medicine man with buffalo power who arranged a circle of buffalo skulls on the ground, sang a song to them, and asked them to get up. The buffalo then arose, but there were now ten times as many buffalo as before.

This legend actually illuminates what has happened to the old animal ceremonialism: it has been reinterpreted to suit the dominant religious pattern, the vision complex. The visionary, the medicine man, the *puhagan*, has taken over the role once played by the master of the species and also the mysterious mechanism we sometimes call magic. The vision complex has grown so strong that it has practically ousted animal ceremonialism and beliefs in supernatural masters of animal species.[16] Even the bear cult has apparently fallen into oblivion. What is left are tales of the bear's mysterious abilities, its strong *puha*, which may turn a man with bear power into a bear, and its granting medical powers.

The rituals that have remained in Shoshoni religion are fairly simple, with the exception of the Sun Dance, which is of course (although some Shoshoni declare the opposite) not at all of Shoshoni origin. It exhibits the lavish Plains ceremonialism, although modified to suit the Shoshoni taste.

Rituals of Human Change: Puberty, Childbirth, and Death

"Rituals of human change," rituals that mark an individual's main life crises, have been called rites of passage by Arnold van Gennep. According to van Gennep, the main phases of each rite of passage are first separation, then transition, then incorporation, and they indicate the individual's passage from one state of existence (or rank, or prestige) to another.[17] Thus, puberty, childbirth, and death are accompanied by rites of passage among the Wind River Shoshoni. Also rituals of disease could be mentioned in this context, but they deserve mention primarily in connection with the medicine men, so their discussion will be deferred.

At puberty there are—or were—different rituals for boys and girls, but both types are designed to secure their transition to adult life with its trials and responsibilities. The boys do not undergo vision quests (as had been the case in Indian cultures in the north and east of the North American continent) but participate in the Sun

Dance, usually on their own initiative. However, today their motives are mainly social: to show other youths their strength and endurance and of course to impress the girls. In a way their present participation in the Sun Dance takes the place of the vision quest as a mark of the attainment of adulthood.

For the girls, puberty officially begins with the start of menstruation,[18] which is considered a state of uncleanliness and very dangerous to men. The menstruating girl withdraws to a brush lodge or (more recently) a wooden shed at a stone's throw distance from the main settlement. She abstains from eating meat but may eat roots and drink water. After a few days or maybe a week, the girl appears again, shrouded in new clothes and painted. One Indian complained to me that this custom is no longer rigorously observed, with the consequence that men no longer receive clear visions and dreams and therefore do not acquire spiritual powers.

The same ritual observances were until recently required of the woman about to give birth. She was supposed to abstain from fattening foods and had to drink hot water. When her time came she moved to the menstrual hut, where she stayed until a month after the birth. She was not confined there but could walk around, although she was not allowed to visit the family quarters. Food was brought to her daily, and she was assisted at the birth by a midwife who had had a dream of serving that profession. The pregnant woman was forbidden to scratch her head with her fingers but could use scratching sticks. She was also instructed not to eat meat. In fact, she mostly subsisted on soups. If the woman ate too much her baby was expected to become fat and lazy.

All these precautions give evidence that a menstruating or pregnant woman is in a dangerous, tabooed state. Spirits avoid her, animals flee from her if she touches them, and men fear her. If a man enters her lodge during menstruation or childbirth, it is believed that he will start bleeding in the nose or the mouth and bleed to death. The woman is on these occasions loaded with electric impurity, as it were, and is dangerous even to herself. At childbirth her balance or purity is restored thirty days after giving birth. She then returns with her baby to her home, and she, her husband, and the baby take a bath in the creek and put red paint on themselves. The paint is considered a blessing.

During the critical times of menstruation and childbirth the husband manifests specific behaviors as a sign of his sharing in the states of his wife and child. While his wife is menstruating, a period that usually spans over four days, he is fasting, restricting his food to bread and water. He also runs several miles a day. The idea seems to be that in this way he contributes to his wife's overcoming the pains and hastens her recovery. This kind of behavior by the husband at childbirth is known in many cultures and is called **couvade.** He consumes light food—but no meat—and drinks much water, evidently to facilitate his wife's labor. As the newborn baby is bathed in warm water, the father dips himself in the cold creek, thus symbolically taking on himself the role of his child. He rises early and moves around, the idea being, said my informants, that as he behaves, so will the child behave in times to come. This parallels the mother's behavior as well: a few hours after the delivery she gets up and starts some easy work, "because she wants her child to become in that way."[19]

The last rites of passage given to an individual are those at death. For two or three days the bereaved cry at the dead person's grave. Women slash their legs and arms with knives so the blood runs; they cut their hair short to the ears and keep it loose. The men cut their hair to the shoulder and untie their braids. The corpse is immediately removed from the *tipi* in which the person lived to a shade, formerly of buckskin, close by. The dead person is painted with the colors and patterns used on festive occasions during his or her lifetime, usually red and white streaks. The painting process is accompanied by a prayer in which the survivors express the hope that the dead person leaves them and does not come back to scare them. The dead person is dressed in his or her best clothes, with some clothing items donated by relatives and friends. A woman is wrapped in her tent cover; a headdress is placed on the head of a dead man. If there are many such headdresses they are placed on trees or sticks in the close vicinity of the grave. All the dead person's goods are distributed among relatives and friends, in particular the horses; but some goods are spared for the grave.

On the third or fourth day after death the corpse is transported to the burial place. Silver dollars are placed on eyes and mouth if these have not been shut. The family tent is buried with the deceased person (and the family moves to another place). For a male the best horse is killed on the spot so that it can serve as its master's mount to the land of the dead; on this horse he hunts buffalo in the beyond. Some of the dead person's belongings are brought to the grave to remain with him or her. A medicine man has his medicine pouch around his neck or packed in a blanket next to him when he is buried; it goes with him to the next world. A woman is equipped in the grave with her kitchen utensils. Finally the corpse is covered with a pile of rocks to protect it from wild animals.

In some cases the crying of the mourners could continue for up to ten days after the burial. Weeping, the women pray that the dead person follows the straight way to the realm of death and does not get lost. Mourning does not cease until after a dance has been arranged one to six months later. On this occasion a specially selected individual paints the bereaved with red and admonishes them to be happy again and join the dance. The mourners abandon the ragged clothes that they have worn until now and don new ones.

These rites of passage go back to very ancient times and express the anxieties experienced by individuals in their fight and concern for fitness and survival and in their fear of death—not of dying, but of the state of death. Such rituals and observances originated long ago in the small hunting societies and were continued by the Shoshoni Indians when they had been transformed into mounted, well-disciplined warriors along the lines of Plains Indians.

The Sun Dance: Thanksgiving Ceremony, Microcosm, Visions, and Curing

The main ritual of the Shoshoni is the Sun Dance. It is basically a thanksgiving ceremony in which the Supreme Being is thanked for the year that has passed and petitioned to guarantee a happy and healthy year to come, a year of plenty. We find such annual thanksgiving ceremonies among many North American tribes. The Great Basin Indians had a simplified version of such a thanksgiving ceremony, and it was preserved among the Wind River Shoshoni until it was replaced by the Sun Dance. (As we shall see, it continued as a Ghost Dance ritual on into this century.) The "Father Dance," as it was called, was a round dance in which men and women formed a circle around a cedar tree, clasping hands and shuffling sideways. Singing, they thanked Our Father for his bounty and implored him to send rain and plenty of food and make the people survive. It is probable, although it is difficult to prove, that the cedar tree represented the World Tree in the middle of the world, the symbol of Our Father's presence.

This ancient ceremony faded into the background when the Plains Indian Sun Dance was introduced about 1820 by the great Shoshoni chief and medicine man Yellow Hand.[20] Of course, the Shoshoni claim that they invented the Sun Dance long, long ago, and other Plains tribes were merely late recipients of this rite. As some elderly Shoshoni remember, it is indeed the other way around. Yellow Hand, who was originally a Comanche Indian well initiated into Plains Indian ceremonialism, transmitted the Kiowa-Comanche type of Sun Dance to his Shoshoni. Since then, the Sun Dance has undergone a series of changes. The Sun Dance that is danced today, usually in July (and nowadays often succeeded by one or two additional Sun Dances in July and August), has been reinterpreted to suit reservation conditions and the impact of Christian ideology. For one thing, prayers for good health and the curing of diseases have emerged as a major concern.

According to Shoshoni beliefs the Sun Dance was initiated by two men, one of them sometimes identified with Yellow Hand, who had sacred visions. These men lived at different times and their visions may be termed the first vision and the second vision. In the legend of the first vision it is said that "many, many years ago" a Shoshoni, some say a chief, was guarding the horses of the camp. He brought them to a butte and sat down there to scout for smoke from enemy camps. As he watched the horizon at sunrise he saw something rushing toward him from the east. Soon he found out it was a buffalo. The man thought it had been scared by hunting Indians. However, the buffalo surprised him by coming close to him. It spoke to him. It told him not to be frightened but to listen to good news. The buffalo said that it had been sent by Our Father[21] to inform the Shoshoni about a way to cure the sick by faith and prayer.[22] The buffalo looked down upon the camp at the foot of the butte and instructed the man how to plan and arrange what is today the first phase of the Sun Dance. Among the many instructions was an order to send out warriors to kill the biggest bull they saw in a buffalo herd. The head had to be severed behind the ears but left joined to a strip of skin along the back including the tail. Nobody was to molest the rest of the body, which was left to the coyotes; in this way the skeleton was preserved.[23] The buffalo head should then be put on a structure during the four initial praying nights of the Sun Dance. The buffalo spirit of the vision said furthermore that Our Father had sent it because the buffalo was the foremost of all animals and superior to them all.

Many generations had passed when there occurred a second vision. This time it was a young man who had a nightly dream of seeing an eagle flying toward him eastward from the sunset and entering his *tipi*. The eagle had been sent by Our Father to instruct the people through the young man to put up a cottonwood pole, fix the buffalo head to this pole, and make a nest for the eagle at the top of the pole. A lodge would then be built around it, and the dancing would take place inside this lodge. This is the second and essential phase of the Sun Dance. The eagle had been chosen as God's messenger because it is superior to all birds, soaring high above them in the sky, a symbol of purity.

The Sun Dance was thus, according to legend, started through visions of supernatural beings, and visions have continued to be part of the ceremony. Many Shoshoni, fatigued by fasting, thirst, and dancing for days, have fallen unconscious or into deep sleep and in this state received power visions. Said one knowledgeable Shoshoni, "Everything we know we have learned through visions in the Sun Dance." It is characteristic that a person who sponsors a Sun Dance should first have a dream of doing so. One may have a nightly dream of an old Indian arranging two sticks to form a cross, or a spirit may tell one in a dream, "You are doing to put up a Sun Dance." Or a voice comes from the Sun Dance hall area admonishing the listener to initiate a Sun Dance. (It may however also happen that a person puts up a Sun Dance after having vowed solemnly to do so, in gratitude for the safe return of a soldier son or as a votive offering for the safe homecoming of a dear person.)

In accordance with the first vision, the so-called buffalo vision, the Sun Dance is begun with a preliminary dance before a skin or brush shelter suspended between four poles set in a row not far from the future dancing lodge. It is July and the grass is in places still very green. One to four men dance here for four consecutive nights, praying to Our Father for protection, health, and happiness. The dancers are usually the sponsor, who is also the main ceremonial leader of the dance, the second ceremonial leader who is a man the sponsor trusts, and one or two other experienced dancers. A fire burns in front of the dancers, who take steps back and forth between the wind screen and the buffalo head. These dance evenings usually end with a cleansing bath.

Thereafter follows the main Sun Dance as outlined in the eagle vision. A company of young men are sent out to bring back a tree to serve as a center pole in the Sun Dance lodge. It has to be a cottonwood tree growing by a stream. The young men find the tree and count "coup" on it, just as in the old days a warrior counted "coup," or points of merit, on the first enemy he could touch with his rod. Special ceremonies are observed when cutting down the tree, which is then carried to the Sun Dance field. Formerly the returning young men were met by a crowd of other young men on horseback, and a sham battle took place between the two groups. However, since there are no more warriors left from the Indian wars, no one has the right to take part in sham battles, so these have been dropped.

When the tree has been brought home, a hole for it is dug in the center of the planned lodge. The buffalo head—now a stuffed head, but formerly a skeleton of a head covered with buffalo skin with sweetgrass in the eyes and nostrils—is fastened halfway up the trunk facing west. The raising of the pole illustrates the emphasis that is placed on ritualism in the Sun Dance: four prayer songs are sung, and four times the pole is raised to the height of the breast, then laid down again. This is done with clapping of hands, singing, and war whoops. Thereafter, eight persons lift the pole again and place it in its hole.

The lodge will now be erected. At a distance of some fifty feet from the center pole and encircling it, twelve sturdy poles are placed. They are connected with crossbeams at the top and joined to the center pole with rafters. One of these rafters has a stuffed eagle at the point where it connects with the center pole. The space between the twelve standing poles is interlaced with cottonwood brush. When finished, the lodge presents an airy building, partly shaded from the sun. This is important for the comfort of the dancers. Their special area is the sacred half circle at the rear of the lodge. During the course of the ceremony the dancers arrange individual booths along the brush wall where they can rest and redecorate themselves (see illustration).

Originally the Sun Dance of the Plains Indians was a ceremony that safeguarded the progress of the coming year by recapitulating and dramatically representing the creation. As far as we know this has never been the Shoshoni interpretation, although during this century the high god's role as creator (for Our Father) has been accepted by some Shoshoni. On the other hand, the idea of the Sun Dance lodge as a replica of the cosmos has been basic to Shoshoni thinking, as will emerge from the following.[24]

Thus it was said explicitly by the Indians that the lodge is sacred because it is a symbol of the world. People coming in to get healed are requested to take off their mocassins and boots. When the Sun Dance is over, the lodge is left to decay—no human agency may destroy it, in any case not the center pole. Here and there on the flats around Fort Washakie old center poles are still standing, monuments of past Sun Dances. The center pole is the most sacred part of the lodge, as we can see from the rites performed around it. It is seen as a communication channel between the people and God, a vehicle for people's prayers, and a source of divine power. It even represents Our Father. At the same time it stands for the Milky Way, the road to the beyond. The forked top of the pole symbolizes the two branches of the Milky Way. Obviously, the center pole is a cultic replica of the World Tree. It has the same function in other Plains Sun Dances.

This interpretation is strengthened by the presence of the buffalo head and the eagle (and eagle's nest) on the pole. The buffalo head,

Buffalo head attached to the top of the Shoshoni Sun Dance lodge. The buffalo spirit stands for food and nourishment and is the chief of all animals.

which reminds the Shoshoni of the first founding vision, represents the game animals and is itself a representative of the foremost game species—the chief of all animals, as one knowledgeable informant assured me. The eagle placed on a rafter at the fork of the center pole is not only the bringer of the "second message," it is the leader of all birds and stands in an intimate relationship to the Supreme Being himself. Sometimes the eagle body is replaced with eagle feathers. The bunch of willows that is attached to the fork of the pole is now the eagle's nest, but was probably originally the grass on which the buffalo feeds. In earlier days it was apparently placed under the buffalo head. At any rate, the buffalo head and the eagle stand for two tiers of the universe, earth and sky. The World Tree penetrates both of them.

In modern times there has been a Christian reinterpretation of this symbolism, so that the center pole symbolizes Christ, the peripheral twelve poles his apostles, the buffalo head the Old Testament and the eagle the New Testament. This is an interpretation that may have appealed to missionaries and Indian agents, but it is void of deeper meaning. It hides the rich traditional cosmological symbolism according to which the Sun Dance lodge with all its details is a microcosmic representation of the world. Prayers and dramatic behavior during the Sun Dance also give evidence that in recent times this old ideological context has been forgotten. The Sun Dance has turned into a ceremonial complex the main concern of which is the restoration of health.

When the Sun Dance lodge stands ready on the day after the last preliminary dance, the families taking part in the ceremony pitch their tents and adjoining arbors in a wide circle around the open place that has the dance lodge as its center. The dancers, all men of varying ages, make themselves ready. They decorate themselves partly with spots of clay, partly with paint. The first day the paint is usually red with black dots on face and arms, the second day yellow. The hair is braided, and in some cases false braids are used with headband and pendants. Occasionally a few feathers may be stuck in the hair of a mature dancer, a sign that he has a guardian spirit. Around the neck each dancer wears an eaglebone whistle with eagle down and a tribal necklace or hanging beads. Eagle down is also attached to the little finger of each hand. The upper body and the feet are naked, while the lower body is covered with a richly decorated apron.

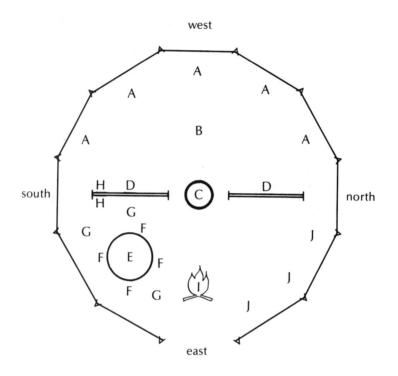

Plan of the Sun Dance Lodge

A   Booths for dancers, separated by saplings of cottonwood or pine
B   Sacred area
C   Center pole
D   Log on the ground separating the sacred area from the rest of the lodge
E   Drum
F   Drummers and male singers
G   Female singers
H   Old men
I   Fire
J   Spectators

We shall now follow the progress of the Sun Dance from day to day.

First day. When the evening star rises over the horizon, the dancers march into the dance lodge in a long row. Their numbers vary, but there may be as many as forty or fifty. They arrange themselves in the back of the lodge. The drummers and the choir of women take their seats in the foreground to the left, as is shown in the illustration on page 72. Standing at the center post, the main ceremonial leader prays to Our Father, a prayer in which his blessing is called down. Then the dancing and singing begin. Each song is repeated four times and finished by whistles from the dancers' eaglebones. The dancing is a monotonous rocking up and down, now and then interrupted with shuffling steps toward the center pole and back again. The dancers turn their faces toward the east. This first evening the dancing is a concerted action by all participants and quite vigorous.

The Shoshoni name of the Sun Dance is "dry-standing-dance." It designates the two most characteristic features of this ceremony, the protracted dancing and the abstention from water. With pauses for rest and sleep, particularly during the night hours, the dancing goes on for the next three days. All this time the dancers are forced to fast and abstain from drinks. Their feet get sore on the sandy and twiggy ground; the thirst, the heat of the day, and the cold of the night are trying. According to old Plains Indian standards this suffering is meaningful: it should make the supernatural powers take pity on the dancers and help them and their people. It is the same technique to win the powers that has been used in the vision quest. Psychologically expressed, it is a technique that stimulates a trance or state of altered consciousness and thus invites visions. Ever so many Shoshoni have acquired their supernatural powers in the twilight states of the Sun Dance.

Second day. At dawn there is sporadic dancing by single dancers or pairs of dancers. Most dancers are sitting shivering in their blankets before a big fire in front of the center pole. At sunrise the dancers form five lines behind the center pole. As the sun appears over the eastern horizon there is intense drumming and whistling, and the dancers stretch their hands towards the red globe. Thereafter they sit down to listen to the leader's morning prayer. This morning ceremony, which is repeated each of the following days, is followed by rest, morning toilet, and repainting.

This day the curing rites begin. About ten o'clock the dancing is resumed on a large scale, and after an hour's dancing, drumming, and singing the persons to be cured appear on the scene. They remove their mocassins and shoes and proceed to the center pole where they are treated by a medicine man, usually one of the ceremony leaders. With the aid of an eagle wing, the medicine man brushes the patients' sore spots, now and then filling his wing with power by touching it to the center pole. Later in the day groups of dancers are blessed by the medicine man in the same way. There is no observable difference between the curing and blessing procedures. They have the same aim: to strengthen the human being with supernatural power.

Third day. This day is said to be the hardest but also the most powerful day. Those who have medicine bags bring them forth, and sacred pipes circulate among drummers and dancers. Most curing rites are performed before midday, that is, while the sun is rising in the sky. The dancing is stronger than ever, and war whoops are heard over the drumming, singing, and whistling. The intense dancing has by now created circular tracks on the ground.

This is the day when sacred visions may appear to dancers. Some dancers are exhausted and lie prostrate on the ground, now and then tended to by the medicine men who massage them. Staggering dancers gaze at the sun or look steadfastly at the buffalo head. Dancers have told me how they have seen the head shaking and steam coming out of the nostrils.

Fourth day. The curing and blessing rites continue. All the dancers appear in turns at the center pole to be blessed by the medicine men, alone or in groups. After noon all curing and blessing activities cease. Instead, again and again announcements are made that money has been donated by cured persons. More and more money is thrown upon a blanket spread out on the ground. Clothes and blankets are also heaped there by relatives of the dancers.

Late in the afternoon a couple of buckets of water are brought in and placed close to the center post. One of the medicine men steps forward to the buckets, faces east, prays over the water, and pours some water on the ground. This is an offering to Mother Earth. The buckets are then passed among the dancers who now rest behind

Opening of the Shoshoni Sun Dance ritual. The leader prays in front of the dancers.

Dancing in the Shoshoni Sun Dance ritual.

Blessing of people in the Shoshoni Sun Dance.

screens in their booths. This is their first sip of water since the dance's commencement. This marks the end of the Sun Dance.

The donated gifts are distributed among the women of the camp. Some blankets are put down at the base of the sacred pole and remain there as offerings to the Supreme Being, an act of gratefulness for his help and blessings.

In the evening there is feasting, round dancing, and war dancing (the Wolf Dance), all dances of social entertainment. However, this concluding celebration, which is attended by all participating families, is very often moved to the evening of the following day.

In retrospect, there is nothing in the Shoshoni Sun Dance expounding the new creation motive, which is so explicit in the Arapaho and Cheyenne sun dances.[25] Maybe the new creation motif was never clear to the Shoshoni or maybe the strong emphasis on curing and reception of supernatural powers after 1890 concealed it (which I find less probable, however). There is a cosmological interpretation implied in the structure of the dancing lodge, as we have seen, but it refers to Our Father as lord of the world, and not to creation.

Curing: Soul Loss and Spirit Intrusion

The concern about curing in the Sun Dance is directly related to the general Shoshoni curing complex. What the medicine men perform in their Sun Dance cures does not deviate from their ordinary methods of coming to grips with diseases; as mentioned previously, their curing activities have been inspired by their guardian spirits.

Among tribal peoples there is a close correspondence between disease etiology—the ideas of the causes of the disease—and the practical treatments of a disease. Whatever the ultimate causes of the disease, whether taboo infringement, sorcery, the wrath of the spirits, and so on, the immediate causes may be defined as **spirit** or **object intrusion** and **soul loss**. If we take a wider comparative view of these diagnoses as they occur among hunting peoples in Eurasia and America, they correspond to two different types of curing practices. Soul loss is usually cured by the medicine man's catching the lost soul and bringing it back to its owner. Object or spirit intrusion, on the other hand, is healed by the medicine man's removal of the foreign body from the patient. However, sometimes in a certain culture one diagnosis becomes dominant or one sort of treatment becomes dominant. In such cases the causal relationship between theory and practice breaks down. The Shoshoni curing complex is a case in point.

In earlier practice the Shoshoni medicine man cured soul loss by falling into a trance. In this state his own soul traveled toward the land of the dead where the lost souls of sick people usually made their way. Such trance expeditions still occurred at the beginning of this century. There are reports of how the medicine man, or shaman, could see his own body lying there on the ground, motionless, while in spirit form he floated away to the other world. Some medicine men could easily visit the land of the dead and return again, provided they did not eat any food there. Others dared not go "over that hill" separating the land of the dead from this world. A lost soul that had passed the boundary line could thus be lost forever.

Soul loss usually refers to a weakening or change of consciousness, such as during high fever or coma. The disappearance during this century of shamanic soul excursions, which my informants described as demanding tremendous power resources not possessed by present-day medicine men, resulted in the application of techniques of intrusion curing to diseases of mind and consciousness. Thus, I was told the following story. An apparently dead child was brought to the medicine man Morgan Moon. Everybody thought that the child was gone for good, but the medicine man said, "No, her soul has just temporarily left the body, but I shall bring it back." Then he touched the top of the child's head, passing his hand over and around it. Suddenly the child opened her eyes and looked at him. The next day she could play again and was completely recovered. Here, as it is in most Native American cultures, the crown of the head is considered the passage by which the soul leaves the body. According to Morgan's surviving sister (whom I interviewed), the presupposition was that the child's spirit had remained in the neighborhood of the body. However, the treatment applied, rubbing the head, is adapted from the technique to cure intrusion.

Today, the very diagnosis of soul loss is gone. All diseases are ascribed to intrusion by harmful objects or spirits. Originally, however, intrusion diseases were deadly diseases, wounds, infections, aches, interior diseases, and so on.

In former days the medicine men had to be invited to come and help in a formal ritual way. In the cases I had the privilege of watching there were no formalities, but much attention was paid to the economic satisfaction demanded by the medicine man.

As is the case in modern professional medicine, the doctor starts by finding out the causes and nature of the disease. (I only know of one medicine man who was supposed to have a precognition of the disease, Tudy Roberts, soon to be discussed.) One medicine man diagnosed the disease by looking through a black scarf, another by seeing with closed eyes. The idea is that the medicine man sees through the patient's body with his interior eye, a sort of X-ray process.

When the diagnosis is made, that is, the supernatural cause has been revealed, the medicine man prays to his guardian spirit to come and help him. An experienced medicine man turns to the particular guardian spirit known to cure the disease that has just been diagnosed. Depending on the type of disease and on the blessings received from the guardian spirit, the medicine man has recourse to different methods to remove the disease agent.

We saw how in the Sun Dance the medicine man brushes the dancers and sick people with his eagle wing. The same method may be used when a patient seeks his help privately. I was told that the feathers draw out the disease object, which the medicine man then brushes away on something in the neighborhood, such as the antlers of a deer running away. In the Sun Dance he puts the disease object on the center pole. Then, when the pole is touched again with the feather wing, the feather wing receives new power, which is then transferred to the patient. Another use of eagle feathers was demonstrated by the medicine man Tom Wesaw. He cured people who had been afflicted with tuberculosis by arrows shot from *nynymbi*'s bow. For this purpose he had recourse to eagle feathers, since the eagle, as we have seen, is *nynymbi*'s enemy. Tom touched the center of the patient's stomach with his feathers, then struck the feathers and, he asserted, felt the little arrow, which he put in his pocket. Then he went out in the dark and blew the arrow away.

The same operation can be achieved with a stick or other object (a buffalo horn, some say). The blowing away of the disease can be a curing method in itself: the medicine man blows on the sick spot through his rolled up fingers. In the past diseases were sometimes blown away to the whites—perhaps to return them to those who had introduced diseases that became devastating epidemics among the Indians.

Another familiar therapy is sucking out the disease. Like the curing by the use of feathers, sucking may also be tried in the Sun Dance. Different medicine men have different ways of sucking. One medicine man put his mouth to the sick spot, sucked, and spat out the evil thing into a vessel. Next, he threw it into the fire. An older colleague of his placed his elbow on the sick spot and sucked at the birthmark he had on the elbow, the idea being that the disease went up into the medicine man's arm and could be sucked out from there. It is difficult for people other than medicine men to see the disease object or disease spirit, but it has sometimes been described as a little being with arms and legs of a finger's length.

The world of the medicine men is best approachable by focusing on one particular medicine man. Tudy Roberts, one of the most respected medicine men, was the head of a family known for its strict adherence to traditional religion and was a Ghost Dance leader in the conservative Sage Creek district. Still, like most Shoshoni, he had listened to what missionaries had to tell, so that some aspects of Christian ideas slipped into his conceptual world.

Tudy was reputed to have received his foremost power, lightning, at the rock drawings, but in direct conversation he denied this. He himself thought that dream visions did not grant sufficient powers—waking visions did. Tudy had experienced several waking visions, but apparently not at rock drawing places. He described and explained these experiences as follows:

Shoshoni medicine man Tudy Roberts.

Our Father above empowered the spirits, those powers which are around us in the country. I have seen them many times: they have their hair braided, tied with strips of skin, and they all appear like Indians, not as animals. Once in a while such a [spirit] Indian appears to me when I am awake, although in a twilight state, not sleeping however. The Indian may also arrive in the dream, but then seems to come in a different way.

Tudy had many spirits of different kinds. He told me that the spirits liked him and that is why they came to him. Other people, he pointed out, were not liked so well by spirits. Only a few persons were as privileged as he was. The following report by Tudy on his acquisition of invulnerability medicine may serve as an example of a traditional dream vision.

I dreamt that I looked toward the east at sunup and saw three bears sitting under some pine trees. I shot at them. One of them approached me and said, "Look now, you see all these bullets twisting the fur here?" "Yeah, I see them," said I. "This is the way I am," said the bear. "The bullets can't kill me." They looked like mud twisted in the fur. The bear said, "I want you to cut off one of my ears, and hang it in a thong at your side. This is the way you should be in the Sun Dance." The dream ended there. Later I found a dead bear, cut off the ear, and wear it now in the Sun Dance. No bullet can kill me. This is true. I never tell lies. That's the way I like to be.

Some dream visions authorized Tudy to initiate and lead a Sun Dance. Sometimes he received supernatural messages affecting other persons. Once in a vision he saw a woodpecker with a pinkish belly seated on the top of the Sun Dance pole singing a new song. The spirit told Tudy to keep this song secret, for one of the younger men would discover it soon and use it. Sometime afterward when the Sun Dance ceremony was held, this young man dreamed about Tudy giving him that song. The young man sang it in his sleep, and upon awakening he went down to the Sun Dance camp, joined the drummers, and introduced the new melody as a song to the American flag. (A flagpole is nowadays raised close to the entrance of the Sun Dance lodge.)

Tudy had secret powers. He knew, in a way that he could not

explain, what the weather was going to be. No wonder, then, that he was counted as a great medicine man by most Shoshoni (although not by the Peyotists, followers of the peyote religion, to whom he did not belong). Many spirits had blessed him with medicine power, the most important of which were the lightning spirits. Once, Tudy told me, he had just finished the Sun Dance and was sleeping on the ground in the foothills of Fort Washakie. In his dream he saw three spirits looking like men and dressed up like the Indians are today, except they wore very clean clothes and had a feather in their hats. They were singing. They were the lightning spirits. They told him to call upon them, "black clouds and lightning," when somebody had been struck by lightning. They would help him doctor the patient. Since that time Tudy had used for his doctoring an eagle tail and an eagle wing with a zigzag mark, made according to the instruction of the spirits. The feathers were hanging on the wall in his timber house. These feathers could also be used for other purposes. For instance, when Tudy did not feel well, he fanned himself with the eagle wing, for the spirits had told him to do so.

Although Tudy had the power to cure diseases like colds, measles, and paralysis, he never cured anybody unless he had received directions to do so in a dream. For instance, if somebody was very badly ill and Tudy was called upon to help that person out, he did not do so until he had prayed for assistance during the night and as a consequence a spirit had appeared and given him the right instructions. The methods used varied according to these instructions. A person with a sore throat was cured by Tudy sticking his finger down the person's throat. In most other cases he used his eagle wing, touching the sick spot with it, drawing the disease out with the wing, and destroying it or blowing it away. For instance, one of my old informants, a woman, had paralyzed legs. Tudy brushed away the "impurity" with his eagle wing, and little by little the old woman recovered. In all cures Tudy started by praying to the spirit helping him and singing a prayer song.

Tudy told me that only he himself could see the disease object. He described it as a round, red thing. If he was unable to extract it in the right way, it would return to the patient. There were diseases that Tudy knew how to cure but didn't do so because he had not received the authorization of the spirits. Wounds resulting from shots by the *nynymbi* belonged to this category. Whatever doctoring

Tudy took on himself, he was humble and straightforward in his attitude and never overcharged his patients. He refused to accept money but gratefully received a blanket or a horse, because the spirits had told him to do so.

As mentioned, Tudy was a prominent member of the conservative Indians of the Sage Creek group. He arranged ghost dances, feeble echoes of the great Ghost Dance at the end of last century. He told me that in the dance he was accompanied by the dead and sang with them. In dreams he had seen the dead, who, he said, look just like ourselves. Since then, old Tudy has gone to live with the dead, forever.

New Religious Approaches

Religion, although conservative, is always changing. Shoshoni religion has changed considerably during the span of time we can view it, that is, since the beginning of the nineteenth century. Influences from Plains tribes were responsible for the creation of the Sun Dance at that time. Influences from Christianity made themselves known at least from the 1840s, possibly earlier, since there was close contact between white trappers and Shoshoni Indians from the 1820s and onwards.[26] Christian influence was strengthened during the course of the century, both directly and indirectly.

In a direct way, Christian ideas entered the Shoshoni scene partly through the French Catholic and Iroquois trappers who had joined the tribe and partly through Catholic missionaries. Already in July 1840 the well known Catholic Father Pierre-Jean de Smet held the first holy mass for Shoshoni Indians close to the town of Daniel, on the upper Green River (the famous La prairie de la messe, "the prairie where Mass was held"). For some time the Mormons exerted a considerable influence, and to this day there are Indians who have been "washed" (baptized), as they say, by Mormons. The introduction of first Episcopalian and then Catholic missions on the reservation in the 1880s contributed to a general spread of Christian ideas, but also to a relativization of the Christian message through the divergent doctrines and rituals of the two churches. In this century also other Christian denominations have appeared on the reservation.

The impact of Christianity is difficult to measure. Certainly practically all Wind River Shoshoni are in some way affiliated with Christian schools or churches. However, at the same time many Indians retain ideas and celebrate rituals belonging to traditional Shoshoni religion. And, as we shall see, a good deal of them cling to new Indian religious faiths. Christian control through the missions has declined in recent times. However, as assimilation to white civilization intensifies, conventional Christianity becomes more accessible as a natural spiritual path.

Indirectly, Christianity has played a role by inspiring new religious movements, on one hand, and by stimulating a partial reorientation of old traditional religious rituals, on the other. The Ghost Dance was one of these new religious movements. It had crystallized out of old traditional and new Christian ideas and received its definitive form in the divine message of a Paiute Indian named Wovoka in Nevada. In visions Wovoka had been informed that the spirits of the dead would return and that the old Indian world would be regained, if people danced the round dance and prayed. This was an attractive message to dispirited tribes that had lost the wars for their land and independence and were now threatened by political, social, cultural, and religious dissolution. Representatives of many tribes, among them Wind River Shoshoni, visited the Paiute prophet and were taught his doctrines. The Ghost Dance spread like a prairie fire among the Basin and Plains tribes in 1890. However, its appearance among the Sioux led to severe clashes between them and the U.S. military. This spelled the doom of the Ghost Dance. It was repressed and survived only on a small scale on some reservations. We have seen how the Shoshoni Tudy Roberts conducted Ghost Dances even in the 1950s. These dances were the last of a great religious movement—and also the last traces of the Shoshoni Father Dance.[27]

Another new religion has been more tenacious, the peyote religion. This is a pan-Indian religion that has grown out of an old pre-Columbian ritual in northern Mexico and southern Texas centered around the small spineless peyote cactus (*Lophophora williamsii*). The believers in peyote's power gather at nightly meetings where they consume the cactus. Peyote is a hallucinogenic (vision-producing) herb and creates feelings of sincere fellowship and solidarity. A peculiar ritual has developed around the eating of peyote. This new religion, which absorbed Catholic concepts and rituals, slowly

spread among the southern Plains Indians in the last century and
was introduced to the Shoshoni about 1919. It now is used by
about 75 percent of the Shoshoni population. On Saturdays the
quick drumming from a lit-up *tipi* or wooden house marks the
presence of a peyote meeting. The drumming, singing, praying, and
consumption of peyote goes on the whole night. Peyotism has ac-
complished what Christianity apparently failed to do—unite the Indians in a church of their own, the Native American Church, and
offer them a faith that satisfies their "Indianness," while providing
relief and meaning in a discordant new age.

At the same time the old traditional religion has continued to
live on, at least in fragments. Its central feature today, the Sun
Dance, is still practiced, although its form has changed as times
have changed. About 1890 its old associations with war were discarded, and it took on the character of a curing ceremony, the details
of which we have seen in the foregoing. At the same time its symbolism began to be reinterpreted in a Christian spirit so that, for
instance, the twelve roof rafters that had been thought to represent
the tailfeathers of the eagle were transformed into a representation of
the twelve apostles of Jesus. Thus Christian ideas were absorbed into
the Sun Dance, changes that certainly pleased the white authorities,
but the basic religious structure was not changed. Finally, the Sun
Dance absorbed older independent rites, such as the vision quest.
Visionaries today receive their supernatural power through the Sun
Dance. Practically all the old beliefs and rituals are now to be found
concentrated in the Sun Dance. We may even talk about a "Sun
Dance religion." Moreover, the Sun Dance is today the main manifestation of Shoshoni tribal cohesion.

Christianity, Peyotism, Sun Dance religion—they are all avail-
able to Shoshoni, whose traditional application of religious com-
partmentalization has taught them to accept the variability of religious forms.

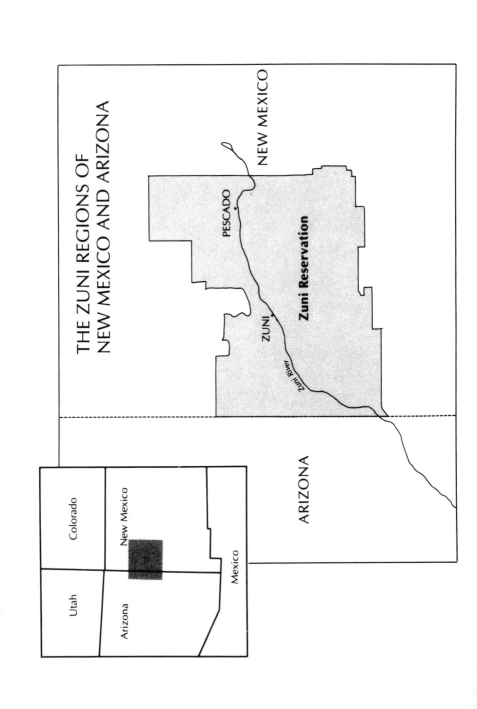

THE ZUNI REGIONS OF
NEW MEXICO AND ARIZONA

NEW MEXICO

PESCADO

Zuni Reservation

ZUNI

Zuni River

ARIZONA

Colorado

New Mexico

Utah

Arizona

Mexico

CHAPTER IV

The Religion of the Zuni: Farming, Masked Dancers, and the Power of Fertility

The Development of Zuni Religion and Culture

Zuni is the name of both an Indian pueblo, or town, and the people of this pueblo.[28] The pueblo of Zuni is situated in westernmost New Mexico, close to the Arizona state line. Its environment could be characterized as a broad valley of high altitude between wooded mountains in the east and arid plains in the west, partly covered by greasewood, yucca, and cactus. The pueblo itself is located on the north bank of the main drainage, the Upper Zuni River. It makes the impression of being situated on a height, for it is built on the mounds of former houses.

Indian neighbors are the once roving Navajo in the north and Apache groups in the south. The closest Pueblo Indians are the Acoma and Laguna in the east. In the northwest, within the boundaries of Arizona, the westernmost Pueblo Indians, the Hopi and their "guests" since the 1680s, the Tewa, have their homes in a series of pueblos. Zuni's rather isolated position in relation to the other pueblos has probably been one of the factors that contributed to its characteristic tendency to combine religious and social organization. Indeed, the Zuni are famous for having constructed the most complex ritual organization of aboriginal North America.

The prehistory of the Zuni is veiled in darkness, but so far as we know, they have always resided in the area where they live today. The Zuni have no linguistic kin. They may have come from the west, as their own traditions tell us, but there is no substantial evidence to support these claims. Proof that the Hopi pueblo of Oraibi has been occupied since 1100 C.E. marks it as the oldest continuously inhabited town in North America, but there are reasons to presume that the Zuni may have occupied their present location even earlier. At any rate, archaeologists have been able to follow an unbroken line of development in this area from the early Basketmaker III times about 700 or 800 C.E. to the later Pueblo eras. These Basketmaker Indians (probably Zuni) cultivated corn and lived in settlements of four or five oval pit houses. About 1000 C.E. these pit houses functioned as ritual meeting places, or **kivas,** while big masonry buildings had taken their place as living quarters. Typical to both house constructions was the entrance through an opening at the top joined to the bottom floor by a ladder. When the Spaniards arrived in 1540 the Zuni people occupied six masonry structures, or pueblos, each one with hundreds of rooms. It is obvious that the period 1000–1200 C.E. when these houses were built marked the transition of Zuni society and religion to greater complexity. The many rectangular *kivas* in close proximity to the houses or even attached to them at this time testify to the growth of ceremonialism.

The history of the Zuni while under Spanish rule is characterized by increasing Spanish influence on administration and religion. The Zuni establishment of a secular administration under a governor and his assistants—all of them appointed by the high religious hierarchy in Zuni—date from this period. The Catholic mission efforts made little progress, although churches were established and saints' fiestas and other festival occasions exerted Catholic influences.

In 1680–92 a general Pueblo uprising against the Spanish meant a major drawback/for the Spanish rule and mission, but also a decline for the Zuni. They deserted their towns in fear of Spanish revenge. When they finally returned, they had decreased in numbers and from that time occupied only one of their old pueblos, which they still inhabit today as Zuni pueblo. In addition, at present many Zuni live in outlying villages close to the farmlands, originally the tribe's summer villages.

When Zuni territory became part of the United States in 1846, a new period of active interaction with the whites began. In 1877 the

United States government established the Zuni Reservation. In spite of pressure first from Catholics and then Presbyterians, the Zuni tended to close the doors to missionary efforts, although they formally accepted Catholic ritualism. There were considerable difficulties with accusations of witchcraft during the last decades of the nineteenth century and the first decades of the present century. When tribal warfare became obsolete, the powerful Bow Priesthood, which was formerly composed of warriors who had taken enemy scalps and had the particular duty of protecting the town from enemies, turned its attention to the persecution of witches accused of upsetting the general welfare of the tribe.

Zuni culture is part of the well-known Pueblo culture of the Southwest, one of the most interesting aboriginal cultures of North America. It is particularly famous for its exquisite art in pottery and silver and turquoise jewelry, its architectural accomplishments, its conservatism that has managed to retain both traditional and spiritual culture, and its beautiful ceremonialism. Basic to this cultural flowering have been the achievements of horticulture and, since Spanish days, sheepherding. Nowhere else in native North America has the tilling of the soil been as intense as among the Pueblo Indians. Not only has this distinctive agricultural practice formed the basis of their economy and sedentary life-style, but it has also been an integral part of their religious beliefs and aesthetic expressions. Their success in keeping out white intruders has enabled them to preserve their ancient traditions intact. Many rituals are still being performed in secrecy and remain unknown to us this very day, although the Zuni and the Hopi are more open in this respect than the eastern Pueblo Indians; for the latter anthropologists have had to resort to more or less clandestine methods of recording beliefs and practices.

There is a cultural boundary between the western and the eastern Pueblos, especially in social and ceremonial respects. (For example, the eastern Pueblo Indians lack clans but are divided into two ceremonial halves or moieties and follow a patrilineal kinship system, instead of the matrilineal kinship system of the western Pueblo Indians.) However, the general cultural picture is very much the same over the entire Pueblo area. The characteristic ethnographic traits are: heavy dependence on maize, squash, and beans, with men as cultivators of the soil; the use of cultivated cotton as textile material, with men weaving cloth on standing looms; habitation in multi-storied and clustered houses of masonry and adobe; and the manu-facture of pottery with polychrome or glazed decoration (red and black among the Zuni) on a whitish ground. Other craftwork in-cludes the production of **kachina** dolls (among the Hopi), silver-work, and the manufacture of turquoise and shell beads (in Santo Domingo and Zuni about 90 percent of Zuni men and women work on silver and turquoise ornaments). Add to this an elaborate ceremonialism with priests, dancers, altars, sand paintings, and masked performances centering around concern for rain and fertil-ity, and we have before us one of the most dramatic and expressive traditions in native North America.

Within this cultural configuration the Zuni hold a prominent position. They are the most populous of the Pueblo nations—they number more than seven thousand; and they are, as said before, the pueblo with the most complex ceremonial organization. To outsid-ers it is also the best known of the pueblos, having been document-ed already in the 1880s by writers like Frank Hamilton Cushing and Matilda Coxe Stevenson and since then intensely analyzed by many anthropologists and scholars of religion.

The sight of Zuni pueblo is presently not as imposing as, for in-stance, the multistoried pueblo Taos or the pueblo Acoma on its high mesa. There was once a mighty town called Halona with ter-raced houses up to five stories on the site where Zuni now stands. Today the houses are single story, built around a plaza. As in some other pueblos the Catholic main church has a dominant position close to the plaza. It was erected about 1699, just after the end of the rebellion, and marks the height of Catholic reconquest, but since that time it has fallen into disuse. Characteristic of Zuni are the small gardens surrounded by walls of stone.

In spite of modernization of living conditions and the introduc-tion of commercialism and higher education, the Zuni hold tena-ciously to their old religion. We know very little about the develop-ment of Zuni religion besides what has been mentioned above. One researcher, Alfred Kroeber, suggests that the concentration of all Zuni to one pueblo in the 1690s meant the rise of the intricate priestly and ritual organization at this time. Earlier, he maintains, the organizational pattern had been less systematized, as in the more easterly pueblos.[29] This is possible. At the same time, there are traces of an even more complex organization in the past. Thus there probably once existed, as among the eastern Pueblos, a sacred moiety organization between a south or summer people, with a Sun Priest, and a north or winter people, with a Rain Priest. There seems also to have been a grouping of clans into major units, so-called phratries, corresponding to the six sacred directions: the four cardinal points, zenith, and nadir.[30] It is thus reasonable to suppose that the complicated ritual system is rather ancient, but that a thorough reorganization and elaboration took place in the years after 1700.

As we shall discover, the outcome of this process is an organization in which different socioreligious groups criss-cross each other: extended family household groups (which are the foundation of Zuni social and ceremonial organization), clans, *kiva* dance groups, rain societies, medicine societies, and priesthoods. All these groups are marvelously integrated into a coherent ceremonial system that makes up the backbone of Zuni religion.

However, no religion is understandable unless it is related to basic principles of faith. Even a religion as expressly ceremonial as Zuni religion has its premises in people's personal religiosity. Dreams and visions sometimes support religious beliefs, although not to the same extent as among the Plains Indians. Due to the highly integrated character of Zuni religion, the ideological premises are given in the myths. Myth and religion form a unit in Zuni religion, the rituals furnishing the practice and the myths the code of religion.

The Structure of Zuni Religion: Emergence from the Earth and the Reemergence of the Spirits

The Myth of Origins

Zuni religious thought takes its departure from the myth of origins. There are two different forms of this origin myth. According to the form known as an **Emanation Myth,** the world emanated from two primeval beings; according to the form known as an Emergence Myth, humankind emerged from the interior of the earth. In fact, the latter account may be considered a continuation of the former. However, during the present century only the Emergence Myth seems to have been known (as reported by recording anthropologists).

The Emanation Myth tells how the Sky Father (or Sun Father)

appeared out of the mists of the primeval world. He cohabited with Mother Earth, and life was conceived in the deepest, fourth womb of the earth. This is what has been called the "world parents myth," known among some Pueblo peoples and tribes in southern California, with analogues in Polynesia and East Asia.[31] It links the origin of the world to sexual procreation and probably is associated with agrarian fertility beliefs.

The Emergence Myth, diffused over large parts of horticultural Indian North America, is definitely part of such agrarian beliefs. The Zuni know it in several versions, but the religiously significant points are roughly the same in all versions. The following is a summary of the Emergence Myth as presented by E. C. Parsons, A. L. Kroeber, and Frank Cushing.

In the beginning the world was empty. Only the Sun Father and Moon Mother were up in the sky, while the people were down in the fourth dark underworld. The Sun asked his two sons, the twin war gods **ahayuta,** to descend there and bring the people up in his light. The two gods, who are described as stars, did so. They instructed the people, who made themselves ready. They took all their sacred bundles for making rain, making snow, and making seeds grow with them and climbed up along a reed (in some versions, using a pine tree as a ladder). They passed through four underworlds, the soot world, the sulphur-smell world, the fog world, and the feather-wing world where they perceived faint light. Finally, they emerged into the bright world of the Sun Father.

There was an old man who was fetched by the two war gods to become **pekwin** (the Sun Priest, the spiritual leader). Spider inspired him to tell the people the identity of the various sacred bundles. Two witches were discovered who said that they had come up from the underworld to kill some people so that the world would not become crowded. They also brought corn of different colors and were therefore accepted. The witches were given a Rain Chief's little daughter to try their powers on. She died and went back to the place of origin. She told two people who came to see her that she would stay there forever and that whoever died would come there.

After this incident the people moved about in an easterly direction, now and then stopping at a certain place for four years before continuing again. At the first stop the people, who had webbed feet and tails, cut their tails off and their fingers and toes apart and thus became human. At another stop the son and daughter of a Rain Chief had incestuous relations with each other and were transformed into clowns, "mudheads." Then they formed two mountains with a river between. When crossing the river many women could not hold on to their small children and lost them. Shortly afterward the people heard singing and dancing from the bottom of a lake: it was their drowned children. The dead children said they would stay there forever, instead of being stationed at the first place of the dead, which was too far away from the living. However, the people continued migrating, and at one place they accepted clan names.

The people then arrived at a place where other beings tried to prevent their passage. Fierce fighting ensued. In their desperation the people turned to the two *ahayuta,* the divine twins of war. The younger twin managed to shoot down the giantess that was leading the enemies, and the war came to an end. And so the tale proceeds until the navel of the world, Zuni, was found.[32]

There are several important observations one can make in connection with this myth. It belongs to the class of Emergence Myths common among southern maize cultivating Indians. Like many other myths, its focus is limited in that it deals primarily with the Zuni (and the Hopi, Havasupai, and Navajo secondarily). What is more important, the incidents of this myth are recited to confirm supernatural validation for rituals and ceremonies, clan organizations, societies, patron animals, and so on.[33] Indeed, depending on the narrator and the situation, particular rituals and sacred objects are emphasized in different myth versions. The most detailed instructions are put in the mouths of the mythical beings. Conversely, deities and spirits that have little or no connection with rituals are scarcely mentioned. The myth is a charter of Zuni rituals.

Zuni myth outlines the major aspects of the Zuni understanding of the nature of the cosmos. In turn, rituals are firmly rooted in Zuni cosmogony and cosmology. This cosmology is closely connected with the surrounding landscape.[34] It was said in the foregoing that the Zuni pueblo is represented as the navel of the earth, the middle around which all cosmic orientation takes place. In ceremonies people observe six sacred points of orientation in the order of north, west, south, east, zenith, and nadir. The six ceremonial rooms, or *kivas,* are correlated with these points, and the fourteen clans are subsumed under them. North is associated with the color yellow and air, west with blue and water, south with red and fire, east with white and earth—associations that have apparently been inspired by heavenly colors and experiences of climate and geography. The zenith is multicolored—the changing sky; and nadir is black—the underworld. As there are four underworlds, there are also four upper worlds, the lowest one for crows, the highest one for eagles.

The Zuni Cosmos

The cosmos, then, consists of four underworlds, a middle world that is the home of the human beings, and four sky worlds. Attention is naturally drawn to the lower worlds, which, in this horticultural society, represent the origins of the human beings. In all horizontal directions the land is surrounded by the ocean, or rather the four oceans, connected with the four cardinal directions. The Sun Father has one house in the eastern and another in the western ocean. The sky is formed like a bowl and is solid. The stars are lights fixed to the sky vault. Apparently there is no observation of the movements of the stars.

In this cosmography the sacred number six appears again and again: there are six directions, and the supernatural beings are connected with them. Thus, there are six places for the rain gods, the lightning and thunder gods, the **beast gods**, the hoofed animal spirits, and so on. Sometimes seven sacred locations are mentioned, the "middle" being added to the other six. However, many supernatural beings are located in the four cardinal directions, and in rituals the most important number seems to be four. This horizontal symbolism means more to the Zuni and other Pueblo tribes than the vertical symbolism among the North American hunting tribes, which focuses on the World Tree.

The sacred geography is oriented around Zuni, or rather, the Zuni center (**itiwana**, "the middle place"). Inside a room in one of the houses there is "the heart of the world," symbolized by an altar containing two columns of rock, one of crystal and one of turquoise. Only the high priest of the foremost Rain Priesthood has access to this center of the world.

The pueblo is spiritually divided into seven parts. The clans are grouped in clusters within these parts, so that "north," for instance, includes all clans with totemic names referring to this direction: the

Crane, Grouse, and Evergreen Oak clans. Several houses contain the sacred medicine bundles the Zuni once brought up from the underworld, according to the myth. These bundles are wrapped around jars with water and seeds, stone images ("fetishes") of beast and prey gods, and masks belonging to the society of masked dancers (*kachinas*). In the storerooms are kept the "corn mothers," the harvested corn ears with the colors of the six directions: yellow, blue, red, white, speckled, and black corn. Zuni as the center of the world thus holds some of the most sacred objects of the universe. Just northwest of the town the Scalp House preserves enemy scalps, which are supposed to promote fertility. These scalps are "water and seed beings" and bestow water, seeds, wealth, longevity, power, and strong spirit.

Spirits and Gods

Many spirits and gods have their residences on mountaintops, in cairns, and in the lakes not far from Zuni. Thus, the *kachina* spirits have their central realm at the bottom of a lake west of Zuni, as the origin myth tells us. People who go there risk their lives, as Stevenson informs us. The twin gods, the *ahayuta*, are celebrated with shrines situated in the close vicinity of Zuni. East of Zuni in the surroundings of the Sandia Mountains lives the lord of the medicine societies, the culture hero **Poshayanki,** who is also head of the beast gods. Unlike most other culture heroes in North America he is the object of worship in a cult. Springs all over the country are the living quarters of the rain gods.

Indeed the supernatural powers are everywhere in nature, a part of the world surrounding humankind. Still, they are different from humans in that they belong to another order of being. The Zuni indicate this by distinguishing the "raw people," the spirits (and gods), from the "cooked people," or "daylight people," the ordinary human beings.[35] The spirits are raw because they eat food that is raw or receive offerings of food that may be raw. Thus, the Zuni throw pieces of food into the fire or on the floor while they say a short prayer. The spirits are supposed to nourish themselves on the spiritual essence of the food. There is however a certain ambiguity in the concept of raw beings. One pioneering investigator, Frank Cushing, thought that the concept stood for game animals, water animals and water sprites, and prey animals and prey gods, but not for other beings. This seems to indicate that the raw beings primarily should be the animal spirits, and that any animal is potentially an animal spirit—you never know whether an animal you meet is a spirit or not—and that any extension of the concept to cover other spiritual categories is secondary. The plain fact is that there is no generic term for supernatural beings.

Nor is there a set of terms corresponding to our distinction between spirits and gods. In North American research it has been common usage to talk about the supernaturals as spirits and reserve the term "god" for the Supreme Being. Students of Zuni religion, however, have called the more important spirits "gods." That rule will be followed here: supernatural beings that have strong ritual functions will be referred to as gods, although the Zuni linguistic usage does not provide for this distinction.

There are, on the other hand, classes of supernatural beings that in Zuni can be comprehended under a single term. One such term is **awonawilona.** The first ethnologists to explore it thought that it stood for the Sun Father or for a bisexual creator. Apparently, *awonawilona,* "holder of the paths of life," is an epithet for two high beings, the Sun Father and the Moon Mother. In the plural it includes a large range of supernaturals. The misinterpretation of a bisexual divinity derives from the fact that both male and female spirits are contained in the collective concept; if the concept is misunderstood as indicating one being, the result is the mistaken notion of one divinity with a bisexual character. The alternate use of a supreme metaphysical concept for a specific divine being and a collective reference to supernaturals in general is well known in other American Indian tribes. (Compare, for example, the term *Wakan Tanka* among Lakota Sioux Indians.)

Father Sun is the paramount figure in the Zuni pantheon, as he is among many Pueblo groups, although among the Zuni's eastern Pueblo neighbors the Corn Mother is the dominating divinity—a not infrequent phenomenon in a matrilinear agricultural community. In Zuni the Sun is the life-giving god, connected with the Dawn People (Spirits of the Dawn). According to one source it was due to his will that human beings came out of the underground. When nobody would give him prayer sticks—short rods with feathers "planted" in the ground to embody a prayer—he sent for human

beings who then ascended from their underworld. Another myth
has it that the culture hero Poshayanki prayed to the Sun to deliver
humankind from the dark world in the interior of the earth. Although the Moon is called "our mother" she is certainly not a sexual
partner of the Sun. She shares however in the cult dedicated to the
Sun. She is reborn each month, grows into maturity, and then
wanes.

The Sun begets offspring with other female beings. The diminutive war gods, *ahayuta*, were born when the rays of the Sun had
penetrated the mist surrounding a waterfall. In mythic times they
were people's helpers at the emergence from the underworld; in our
own days they are the source of wind and snow. They live on the
mountaintops where people have erected their shrines. The myths
describe them as playful little boys ready for mischief of all sorts,
obscene and ridiculous, but they save humans from monsters—they
are simultaneously culture heroes and tricksters in the same form.

Other beings also figure as culture heroes. One of them is Poshayanki, "the wisest of men," who once instituted the medicine
fraternities. He is thought to have implored Sun to save humankind
from the underworld, in some versions of the Emergence Myth. Another culture hero is **Payatamu,** who taught the people to cultivate
corn and then disappeared. He is connected with the myth of the
flight of the Corn Maidens (see below). His flute is the male sexual
symbol.

In the sea and underground waters dwells the water serpent, conceived of as a plumed or horned snake. This monster can bring rain
and may impregnate bathing women. He controls floods, land-
slides, and earthquakes. Powers of rain and dew are the **uwanammi,** who live along the ocean shores and in springs all over the
country. They travel as clouds and patches of fog. Some of them are
responsible for lightning and thunder. As gods of the rain they do
not stand alone, for most Zuni supernaturals are rain makers. Also
the *kachina* spirits bring rain when they leave their abodes in the
lake "whispering spring" west of Zuni and appear as clouds. The
kachinas, or **koko,** are the spirits of the dead who, like the dead in
other horticultural religions, further fertility through the life-giving
rains. Also the spirits of the dead enemies, through the preserved
scalps, bring rain. There are indications that some of the *uwanammi*
are ancestors, like the *kachinas,* but the two categories are obviously

otherwise not identical. Indeed, the ancestors seem to form a vague collectivity of spirits that are identical with several spirit categories, but more generally with *kachinas.*

Hunting and Animal Spirits

Some of the supernaturals, and also some of the *kachinas,* supervise hunting and game animals. Considering the emphasis placed on agricultural pursuits, it may seem surprising that hunting is at all tied to Zuni religion. But we must remember that the hunting substructure of American Indian cultures is conspicuous within the life of all tribes and that the hunt is a subsidiary economic pursuit in Pueblo culture. Therefore, it is to be expected that clear traces of the old hunting ideology are found among the Zuni. They are careful to see that the bones of slain animals are not molested, they honor the dead animal with blankets and jewelry, and their designs of animals on pottery and symbolic shields belonging to the priesthoods display a line drawn between mouth and heart—the "lifeline" of the animals.[36]

The ancient heritage of hunting and its continued importance explains the belief in animal spirits among the Zuni. One category of animal spirits is the beast or prey gods, which are the masters or patrons of animal species. Foremost among them is the Mountain Lion, guardian of the north (for he is yellow, the color of the north). Next in rank come the Bear, guardian of the west, the Badger, guardian of the south, the Wolf, guardian of the east, the Eagle, guardian of the upper regions, and the Mole, guardian of the lower regions—all of them colored or speckled in a way that associates them with the respective regions. However, in line with Zuni religious organization, these prey gods are subordinated to Poshayanki, the chief of the twelve medicine societies, and are his personal guardians. In other words, the representatives of hunting culture and untamed "nature" have been organized into the socioreligious system of the urban, agricultural Zuni. Animal spirits have also assumed healing functions in addition to their old functions of providing good luck in hunting. The latter functions have been eclipsed by the former. Animal spirits have also become gods of magic and witchcraft.

Another category of animal spirits are the masters of the "hoofed game animals." They are also arranged according to the sacred directions, although their numbers have been expanded with other game lords to make up the necessary six varieties: the Mule Deer in the north, the Mountain Sheep in the west, the Antelope in the south, the Whitetail Deer in the east, the Jackrabbit in the zenith, and the Cottontail in the nadir. There is also mention of a mother of all game animals who furthers their propagation and who lives at a place south of Zuni. This tradition is obviously in conflict with another one, according to which dead game animals go to the great *kachina* village at the bottom of the sacred lake west of Zuni and are restored there. Not unexpectedly, therefore, this mother of the game is represented as an enemy of the lake *kachinas*.

Farming and the Corn Maidens

While the animal spirits or gods are important as mediators between the medicine societies and the culture hero Poshayanki, the spirits of earth and vegetation are directly related to horticulture. Thus we turn again to Mother Earth, who in the Emanation Myth is described as a sexual partner of Father Sun. In general beliefs she is always recognized as a vague personification of the earth and its growth. As we have noted, the four underworlds are her wombs. The Zuni pray to her in wintertime "that our earth mother may wrap herself in a fourfold robe of white meal, that she may be covered with frost flowers." Then comes spring "when our earth mother is replete with living waters," and the Zuni pray for summer, or

> That our earth mother
> May wear a fourfold green robe,
> Full of moss,
> Full of flowers,
> Full of pollen.[37]

The flowering season is a work of many forces in addition to Mother Earth—the rain and thunder gods, the *kachinas*, the water monsters, and of course the lifegiving Father Sun. The most important aspect of vegetation, maize, is of many different colors, all personified in the Corn Maidens. Also in this case the spiritual beings are vaguely identical with their plant forms, the corn. The corn plants have been described as personified beings whose tassels are their heads and who hold the maturing corn ears in their arms. This treatment of earth and corn as live forces is a good illustration of the way the Zuni combine the spiritual and material.

These identifications between spirit and matter may make us wonder whether the general division between this world and a world of another order is applicable here. The answer to this question is that we must not expect strict conformity to abstract logic by American Indians. In principle the Zuni maintain a distinction between the two worlds; in practice the boundary between the two worlds is often disregarded as a result of the human tendency to give concrete form to religious concepts: in this way they become more realistic. Earth and corn are more palpable substances than sky and ethereal ghosts; therefore they give a more "realistic" impression. This is further complicated by the fact that Zuni religion tends to combine the spiritual and the material in ritual performances and mask ceremonialism.

The Corn Maidens are a good example of Zuni myth and ritual: they are the main persons in a dramatic myth describing (like some ancient Near Eastern myths) the flight of the fertility and vegetation goddesses from the lands and their return. There are many versions of this myth in Zuni, but they are similar in their general structure and course of events.[38] The myth recounts how the Corn Maidens are insulted by the people in their storerooms—they are not cared for or even assaulted by a man who is described as a Bow Priest or as one of the divine twins. (This really means the same thing, for the *ahayuta* are the supernatural counterparts of the Bow Priests.) As a result, the Corn Maidens flee the land, or at least hide themselves under the wings of ducks (in the ocean), causing a famine. The people send out messengers to find the vegetation goddesses. In one version the seeker is the culture hero Payatamu, the initiator of the corn cultivation. This handsome flute player, patron of the Flute Cult associated with one of the medicine societies, recovers the Corn Maidens and lures them back to the people. They consent to "give their flesh" to the people, and the famine is over.

Like other Zuni myths, this corn myth is dramatized in ritual: in the Thlahewe ceremony (a corn ceremony every four years), in the harvest rituals each fall, and in the **Shalako** ceremony in wintertime. On these occasions the Corn Maidens are impersonated, or their corn ear representatives are treated like persons. It is interesting to note that the Zuni are reluctant to sell corn from their homes, because they fear that all their corn may follow what is sold, exactly as the stored corn in mythical times followed the fleeing Corn Maidens.

There are other female spirits as well that play a role in the life of the Zuni Indians. For instance, the maker of Zuni prayer sticks—short rods with feathers that are "planted" in the ground to embody a prayer—calls on the three "mothers" Clay Woman, Black Paint Woman, and Cotton Woman. These spirits help him in turn to tie the cotton around the stick and to "clothe the plume wands with their flesh."[39]

The remarkable thing about all these divinities and spirits we have just reviewed is that they are integrated into some ritual: all these divinities and spirits have their main function in these rituals rather than appearing as beings who reveal themselves out in nature or in people's dreams. With only slight overstatement we could say that the spirits are primarily important in relation to the ritual aims they fulfill and to the ritual organizations they preside over and protect.

An example of this integration is the connection between sacred time, rituals, and spirits—what is usually called the calendar round. As in other Native American cultures, the Zuni have a time concept according to which year follows after year, season after season, in what some scholars have called an "undulating" or cyclical pattern. It is true that in modern times a more linear concept of time has been recorded, manifested in ideas that at the end of the world all things made by humankind will rise against them and hot rain will fall. However, such ideas obviously have originated in Western (and Christian) notions of a final catastrophe. The typical agricultural time pattern is the cyclical pattern, and this seems to be an ancient form with the Zuni.

This pattern takes its beginning each year with the rituals for a successful corn cultivation and therewith a healthy and happy life for all Zuni. The year ends when the powers of fertility have been exhausted and have to be renewed. It is thus a matter of a sacred year, with a calendar of festivals and rituals closely correlated with the growth, maturing, and harvesting of the grain. We have here clear parallels to the agricultural calendars in Europe and Asia. Like other Pueblo tribes, the Zuni divide their year into two halves, one period between midwinter and midsummer, and another period from midsummer to the following midwinter. The first period is marked by cleansing rituals and ritual dances to ensure growth and flowering. The second period is dedicated to rain promoting ceremonies, so that the harvest will be assured. We may conclude that the two seasons of the calendar year are ecologically adjusted to the welfare of the maize and, accordingly, to the lives of human beings. (A more detailed account of the progress of the ritual year will be given in the next section.)

Kachinas

The main spirits figuring in this calendar are the *kachinas,* Zuni *koko.* "Kachina" is actually a Hopi word and is the general term by which all spirits of this kind among Pueblo peoples have come to be known to the outside world, so it will be used here to refer to Zuni spirits. *Kachinas* are, in Zuni thought, all "masked" beings, that is, all those spirits that can be impersonated in ritual dances with masks. The *kachinas* serve many purposes. They are, among other things, cloud and rain makers who approach the pueblo in the form of ducks. They come from the mountains or from the *"kachina* village" at the bottom of the sacred lake southwest of Zuni, which is the home for most of them.

This area is also the home of the dead, or rather, those dead that have been initiated into the *kachina* society—and, as we shall see, the majority of all men belong to this society. At death, the corpse is buried in the churchyard with its head to the east. For four days the spirit of the dead person lingers. During this time his surviving spouse fasts and purifies herself by scattering cornmeal. When the fourth day has gone the dead person turns into a *kachina* and departs for the sacred lake, while the bereaved burn his personal property.

Scholars have discussed whether the *kachinas* were originally the dead or the rain spirits. We know from other horticultural peoples that there is a tendency to identify ancestors with fertility spirits. Scholars have pointed out that in Pueblo culture the idea of fertilization dominates practically every area of thought and that therefore the spirits of the deceased were interpreted in conformity with this pattern.[40] As we have noted, among the Zuni most groups of spirits, including the *uwanammi,* the water monsters, the *kachinas,* and even the enemy scalps, may send rain. The *kachina* complex also may have outside influence. There is evidence that this particular form of *kachina* worship was introduced from Mexico, perhaps not so very long ago.

There are among the *kachinas* three categories of deceased persons. First, there are those who have recently died. They may or may not produce rain. Second, there are the ancestors who have been dead for some time. The Zuni pray to them for health and survival, rain, and a good corn harvest. Third, there are the original *koko,* the children who died by drowning after the Emergence and apparently also those who died and went back to the underworld. Sometimes all three categories are termed *koko;* sometimes people make a distinction between ancestors and *kachinas.* Apparently only those who in life were members of the *kachina* society, especially those who have been officers in the society and bring their own masks, go to the *kachina* village where they are welcomed. Members of the rain priesthoods join the *uwanammi,* and distinguished members of other priesthoods and societies join their respective spiritual protectors in the other world. What happens to women and children is not always clear. On the whole, the picture of the destination of people after death is quite varied and confusing. This is not surprising, because most beliefs about the afterlife among American Indians are ambiguous and even contradictory. Besides, the Zuni are known to observe ritual details more rigorously than matters of belief and to pay less attention to concepts about an afterlife.

The conditions after death, as far as they are known, are described in rather positive terms. Husbands and wives (to the extent that they get along) live together in the *kachina* village, but there is some doubt whether their young deceased children can join them; it is sometimes said that these children turn into water animals. As *kachinas* the dead spend a happy time in their underwater realm. They are beautifully dressed and adorned with beads and feathers— just like their masked human representatives on earth. They dance and sing and feast. If they wish, they may visit their living kin. They do that now and then, arriving in clouds. It is said that at the beginning of time they often came to dance in the plaza of the pueblo. However, because on their return to the *kachina* village they happened to take somebody back with them to the other world (that is, the person died), they decided "no longer to come in person." Instead, people were told to imitate their costumes and dances, and they would be with them in spirit. They have done so ever since. The *kachinas* come flying to Zuni in the shape of ducks, and the members of the *kachina* society impersonate them by dressing up in their costumes, particularly their masks. The impersonators have to make food offerings before they can put on the masks. It is said that when the dancer dons the mask he is assisted by the invisible *kachina* spirit who stands behind or in front of him. After the performances, the spirits return to their village, again in the guise of ducks.

We have here another testimony of the close integration between religious concepts and rituals in Zuni: in this case it is the dead ancestors who play a part in rituals. In fact, the Zuni *kachina* cult is the most conspicuous example of ancestor worship in North America. The Hopi are also famous for their *kachina* cult, but the associations between the dead and the *kachinas* are not as concrete there as they are among the Zuni.

In view of this ancestor worship it seems strange that the name of a person who has died is taboo. The explanation could be that the dead person, tabooed because of his or her dangerousness, loses individual identity and goes up in the great collectivity of *kachina* spirits. When the Zuni turn to the *kachinas* in prayers and throw sacrificial food to them in the Wide River, west of the town (the food is thought to be carried by the river to the sacred lake where the *kachinas* have their home), it is to the ancestors as a whole that the Zuni direct themselves, not to individual ancestors.

As often is the case in Native American beliefs about life after death, the Zuni believe the dead will die again. There are different views of what then happens to them. Some people apparently hold that for each death a dead person descends deeper into the underworlds, finally reaching the fourth underworld from which the first ancestors once emerged. Thereafter the person transmigrates into an animal, the nature of which is decided by the individual's activities in this life. Thus, a witch may become a coyote, lizard, bullsnake, or owl, all detested animals, whereas a prominent member of the *kachina* society turns into a deer.

The Zuni Version of the "Orpheus" Tradition

The Zuni, like many peoples of North America, tell versions of the touching story of how a man tries to follow his dead wife on her way to the realm of the dead to bring her back to life again. (This story, reminiscent of the Greek tale of Orpheus traveling to the underworld to find his dead wife, is sometimes called the North American Orpheus tradition.) In the American tradition the story often gives the impression of being linked to experiences in trance or deep sleep, but whatever the background, this tale supplies us with some interesting details of Zuni notions of the afterlife. It relates how a witch girl, overcome by jealousy in her love for a young hunter, kills the man's young wife. The wife is buried, and her husband sits mourning at her grave. After dark he sees a light at the grave. His wife talks to him: "My husband, do not sit facing the west. You are not dead yet. Face to the east. I am still here in this country. On the fourth day I shall go to Kachina Village." The hunter tells her that he wants to go with her. She agrees he can go with her but instructs him to dress in his best clothes, as if for a funeral, and to bring along extra moccasins, four pairs, and a downy eagle feather to tie in her hair. He does as she says, and early in the morning of the fourth day he has everything ready. He ties the eagle feather to the crown of her head, and she tells him to follow the feather. They start their way westward, crossing large fields of cactus. She moves swiftly (she is a spirit), but he gets tired and wears out his moccasins, one pair after another. After some time they arrive at an open country without cactus and come to a chasm. He sees the feather way down below but cannot follow it anymore. As he stands there crying, a squirrel turns up and offers to help him. He climbs onto the squirrel's back and is carried down the canyon and up the other side. As he turns around and looks back, he cannot see any chasm. He then continues walking. Soon he sees the feather far ahead at the bottom of a big cliff. He cries, and again a squirrel comes to his rescue and carries him down the cliff. As he looks back he does not see more than a plain. He continues on his path, but in the long run loses track of the feather. He cries, for he loves his wife. Nevertheless, he goes on and finally catches sight of the feather. At the end of the day he discovers the *kachina* village. His wife tells him to wait outside of the village for four days, because he is not dead yet. She goes into the lake, while her husband sits there weeping. "And that is why, when a husband or wife dies, we tell the one who is left not to weep or he will die soon."[41]

This Orpheus tale does not correspond exactly to the general pattern of North American Orpheus tradition, because the question of the return of the dead woman is not answered. However, the tale does illustrate some basic Zuni concepts about the dead. Thus, the dead do not depart for the underworld until four days after the time of death. They go west, traveling on this earth, but are invisible; only the feather on their heads belonging to this world can be seen. The dead can traverse obstacles the living cannot, and they are not hurt by the cactus on the way. From the quarters of the other world, canyons and mountains do not look like obstacles on the path. Only a really dead person can penetrate the lake of the *kachinas*.

These ideas about the dead are confirmed in the myth of the Emergence, in which it is maintained that the dead have no bodies, they are like the wind, and they take form from within of their own wills. At the same time they have a part in the common life within the world. Wind is identical with breath, which is the symbol of life. At the end of a prayer or a chant, people inhale as an act of ritual blessing. We have noticed that the feather is a visual manifestation of breath. This idea is common in Native culture and religion.

Structure Summary: Mythical Emergence and Ritual Reemergence

Zuni religion, like Shoshoni religion, is not codified as a written theology, but in comparing the two traditions, the Zuni heritage is more concisely formulated in the myth of origins and more uniformly carried out in the collective rituals. One reason the Zuni have a more clear and compact religious system is that they have lived in the same general area for many centuries and have been able to retain a rather unbroken line of beliefs and practices. The farming culture of the Zuni has been the material foundation of a rich religious life permanently settled at and around the present town of Zuni.

The myth of origins sets the tone for most Zuni religious concepts with the notion of the emanation of the world from the primeval parents Sky Father (or Sun Father) and Mother Earth: as a result of their cohabitation, life was conceived within the deepest womb of the earth. Another version of the myth of origins depicts the emergence of people from within the womb of the earth. This myth, or pair of myths, reveals an interesting aspect of the Zuni spiritual world. Of the many spirits or "gods," Sun Father is the most important figure in the pantheon, but more attention is paid to the earth and female forces of fertility. Indeed, the most important spirits are the *kachinas,* and the *kachina* dances in the Shalako ceremony are the main annual religious performances because they depict the annual reemergence from the earth. In other words, Sky Father (or Sun Father) was important in the origin of the cosmos, but power is concentrated mainly in Mother Earth and fertility. This power is seen in the maize and in the Corn Maidens: we can talk of the Corn Maidens being embodied in the maize, or the corn plants as personified Corn Maidens. In fact, there is a separate myth to account for the gift of corn to the Zuni by the Corn Maidens, who then are offended and leave the land, later to be persuaded to return to Zuni with their blessings of corn.

Such myths can be seen as the foundation of ritual; but because of the dominant role of collective rituals in Zuni religion, it is also possible to see ritual as the justification for retaining the myth. What is important in the structure of Zuni religion is the close integration of myth and ritual, with all ritual grounded in mythical tales. Indeed, the masked dancers of the Shalako represent an annual reemergence of power from the world and a renewal of time and the world for the Zuni. As we shall see later, time, or the annual ritual year, is divided into two halves by the winter and summer solstices; the Shalako at the winter solstice marks not only the seasonal turning back of the sun but also the ushering in of the new year by masked gods. The myth of origins lays down the precedent for sacred time and also establishes the site of Zuni as the center of the world, or sacred space. The Zuni pueblo (or town) is seen as the navel or middle of the earth, and all cosmic orientation takes place around this center. For the Zuni this means not just the four cardinal directions, but the sky (zenith) and especially the underground (nadir). The *kiva* is the ceremonial room of the Zuni imitating this cosmic model, including the *sipapu* or hole of emergence. Just as the Sun Dance lodge represents a microcosm for the Shoshoni, the *kiva* is a miniature cosmos for the Zuni.

The heart of Zuni religion is the elaborate ritual life of interrelated ceremonial societies and groups, each with its own set of rules for membership and procedures. The careful conformity to ritual precedents may make Zuni religion appear to be mere mechanical performance, but we should not lose sight of the thrust of all these activities, which is to bring the individual and the group in conformity with the spirit of the universe. Zuni see their participation in the rituals as part of a larger drama in which they come into harmony with the universe. Some of the obvious intentions of these rituals are to assure the fertility, growth, and harvest of maize in its various stages, as well as thanksgiving. But for the Zuni the growing of maize is not simply a means of making money, it is a way of life, a way of taking part in the drama of the emergence and reemergence of plant and animal life. We have seen that for the Shoshoni the ideal of religious life is the intense personal vision; the vision is the goal of much religious activity, especially the Sun Dance, and visions are the authority and sources of new ritual. Among the Zuni the ideal religious life is more a submersion of the individual in the group ritual activity, such that all work together in unison with the rhythms of the cosmos. Indeed, a person who acts too much on his or her own is thought to be using religious power for evil intentions and may be accused of witchcraft. (Witches and witchcraft will be discussed in the next section.) Zuni emphasis on collective ritual even spills over from this life to the next, for all Zuni men belong to the *kachina* society, thus assuring their permanent abode in the "*kachina* village" at the bottom of the sacred lake near Zuni.

The Dynamics of Zuni Religion: Harmony with the Cosmos Through Collective Ritual

Religious Societies and Collective Ritual

Ruth Bunzel, a leading scholar and writer on Zuni culture and religion, writes about the Zuni male: "the only sphere in which he acts as an individual rather than as a member of a group is that of sex."[42] Indeed, a Zuni man is normally a member of several ritual organizations and disappears, as it were, behind the collectivistic ritual machinery. This is the background of Ruth Benedict's famous characterization of the Zuni as Apollonian, in Nietzsche's sense, with a sober faithfulness to tradition and a playing down of the individual and personal experiences. Benedict's portrait of the modest, unassuming Zuni personality has been challenged and is certainly exaggerated, as we shall soon see, but it contains some elements of truth. There is no doubt that conformity to traditional customs and usage and adherence to established ritual practice are esteemed virtues in Zuni society: these virtues constitute the "ideal personality type." A person with these qualities keeps the life-sustaining and cosmically important rituals going, thereby preserving Zuni life both in its worldly and in its metaphysical dimensions. Every person has his or her place in the rich and complex ritual apparatus, and everyone is expected to do his or her share.

Those who openly violate this order or code of ethics or are even accused of going against it jeopardize their social reputation and even their lives. They may be accused of witchcraft. This happens, for instance, if a person is suspected by the relatives of a deceased Zuni to have caused the latter's death. According to general belief, all diseases that are not the result of an accident are due to the evil operations of witches. It is the task of the Bow Priests to find out whether the accusation is justified. Not so long ago they did this by relying on torture to extort a confession from supposed culprits. The arms of the suspects were crossed behind their backs, and they were suspended by their thumbs or wrists to a beam of the church wall. They might hang there for several days without food or drink, now and then knocked and kicked by the priests. Witch trials could end in expulsion from Zuni or even in execution. In later times flogging has also been a form of punishment.

For the well-behaved male Zuni, the best proof of his unassuming and loyal character is to join a good number of the societies and cult associations that are at his disposition. Membership in these organizations may come about through recovery from an illness, distinction in war, and individual choice. In some cases they are restricted by clan affiliation. Indeed, what we have here is an intricate system of social and ceremonial connections, in which different principles of order interlock with each other in a bewildering complexity.

We have first of all the kinship ties. The Zuni reckon kinship on the mother's side and belong from birth to the mother's clan and household. To some extent these matrilineal connections determine the positions of office that an individual might hold in the religious system. However, this structure is complicated by a man's being at the same time "child of the father's clan," for he also has responsibilities to his father's clan, although these are less important positions.

In the past there were a great number of clans. Today, however, there are fourteen clans, all matrilineal, all exogamous. Indeed, Zuni even avoid marrying a spouse taken from the father's clan. Each clan is totemic, that is, it has a clan emblem that is usually an animal or a plant. For instance, we find Eagle, Turkey, Bear, and Deer totems and Dogwood, Corn, Tobacco, and Mustard totems. There is, however, no real cult of these totems and no concept of spirits behind them. The clans have the right to place their members into the rain priesthoods. These are important offices and represent the highest positions a Zuni can attain as a member of a clan.

Next, we have what could be called the free associations. Memberships in *kiva* groups and medicine societies are based on a variety of reasons, such as individual choice, paternal choice, or recovery from a specific illness. However, such a membership may be limited by clan affiliations, as noted above.

A third category is war achievements. Male Zuni who have taken scalps are introduced into the Bow Priesthood. We may of course wonder how this priesthood could still exist today, when there is no tribal warfare. It seems that veterans from the two World Wars, the Korean War, and the Vietnam War could take on the roles of Bow Priests but rarely have done so. These modern wars lack the ritual values of the old tribal wars.

We have so far talked only about the men. In many respects they are dominant in the ritual life, although women certainly have access to medicine societies and some priesthoods. The emphasis on males ties in with their economic dominance: the man is the cultivator of the soil, the builder, and the weaver. This is a pattern that was also practiced in pre-Columbian Mexico and is no doubt related to the incipient urban civilization there. Where the man's ancient role as hunter has fallen away, as was the case in classical Mexico, his activities are transferred to the main economic activity, horticulture. Here we face another hint of the strong impact of ancient Mexico on Pueblo Indian culture.

On the other hand, women play important roles in other connections. The housewife, with her mother, brothers, and sisters, owns the family rooms, and she and the other women of the family are rulers there. The husband is a guest in her home and may be dismissed when she so wishes. To her belong also the sacred fetishes, a most precious part of Zuni sacred paraphernalia.

Having discussed the rules of joining the ritual societies, including the woman's part in the social and ceremonial system (which, it must be stressed, in many respects constitutes a unit) we shall now turn to a presentation of the most common and most important religious and ceremonial organizations.

Ceremonial Organizations

The *kachina* society. All young males, but very rarely girls, are introduced into one of the six "*kiva* groups" that exist in Zuni. Usually the parents decide which *kiva* group a child should join. Later in life the initiated may change to a *kiva* group of his own choice. The initiation is spread over two periods. Sometime between the ages of five and nine the child undergoes a preliminary initiation in the *kiva*. He is whipped by masked *kachinas,* probably for purifying reasons or, as it is expressed, "to take away the bad luck." (Whipping is never used as a means of punishment.) The whole ritual signifies that the young child is put in the charge of the *kachinas*. The second, final initiation takes place between the ages of ten and twelve years. The children are then whipped a second time and taught the secrets of the *kachina* ritualism.

The *kiva* groups represent the *kachina* society. This all-embracing society is headed by a chief who always belongs to the Antelope clan. His deputy or "speaker" is a member of the Badger clan. Two Bow Priests also belong to the "board." The rituals of the society are, as always in Zuni, characterized by prayers, chants, and dramatic performances. Symbolic actions and objects such as the offering of corn meal and prayer sticks are frequently used.

Each *kiva* group is bound to a particular *kiva*. As said before, the six *kivas* are modeled on the four cardinal directions and the zenith and nadir. The *kivas* are usually rectangular rooms in the house units and are situated above ground, not subterranean as among the eastern Pueblo peoples. There is a ceremonial order to the *kivas,* so that each season the dances begin with the *kiva* on the main plaza and then continue in a counterclockwise direction among the other *kivas*. The performances in the *kivas* are secret. We know that rehearsals take place there and also purifications when some sacred matter has been defiled. The splendid *kachina* dances and shows that take place on the plaza and are open to the public will be discussed later.

Medicine and hunting societies. These are twelve societies into which men and women who have fallen ill and been treated by members of a medicine society are recruited. Indeed, anyone who has received such treatment is required to join the society; otherwise his or her life is in danger. The medicine society is a secret society that a person may enter only after expensive gift feasts. The initiation ceremony takes place under the supervision of a "ceremonial father" who is the person who cured the individual. In a few of these societies it is customary or even demanded that the leading members of the society belong to certain clans. Women who have been recruited may not appear in more advanced curing functions.

The medicine societies have as their patrons the beast gods for whose cults they are responsible. These gods are the givers of medicine and long life, but also of witchcraft. The most powerful of the gods is Bear, the god of the west. In the Bear Dance the dancers have bear paws attached to their arms, growl like bears, and dash about wildly as if possessed by bears. In other words, they impersonate the bear. This is interesting, for over large parts of North America the bear is the particular guardian spirit of healing medicine men. The Zuni have apparently taken over the ancient function of the individual bear medicine man and collectivized it into a group of bear medicine men.

Characteristically, members of the medicine societies remove the disease object by sucking, as is the case among native medicine men in most of North America. Furthermore, the different medicine societies are experts about particular kinds of diseases and hold rituals featuring altars, fetishes, and other sacred things. Each society has its peculiar fetish, kept by the main household of the associated clan. In addition, each member of the society has his or her own personal fetish, a feathered ear of corn, placed on the altar. All this reminds us of the functions of individual medicine men in other areas and of their ritual paraphernalia. In other words, the medicine society is a corporation of medicine men and women, but these have not gone through the guardian vision quest and they do not perform curing while in a state of trance. This is a typical case of Pueblo collectivization: we see in these medical practices the attitudes of a hunting people expressed in the collective form of horticulturalists.

Another interesting item is the connection between these societies and hunting. For instance, the members of the Coyote Society formerly took part in the communal rabbit hunts. They are said to be good deer hunters and cure all illnesses thought to be caused by the deer. The emphasis on male pursuits in this society explains why no women are allowed membership. In most other medicine societies women are welcome, although they are not allowed to hold office.

The combination of medicine for curing and medicine for hunting echoes the characteristic capabilities of American Indian medicine men in hunting societies, for instance, on the Plains. However, the extreme individualism of these doctors has no counterpart in Pueblo culture. It is noteworthy that practically all medical practice in Zuni is in the hands of the medicine societies.

These medicine societies are very active in cultic and ceremonial practices. The time for their regular performances is fall and winter. At the winter solstice the initiated have their retreats in their sacred houses (not *kivas*) to make prayer sticks for the ancestors and to pray for rain and fertility. Thereafter, they call on the beast gods and demonstrate to the public their powers of curing. They also appear publicly now and then when there are occasions of curing or initiation. Members of other societies are often invited to be present at the ceremonies.

The Rain Priests (**ashiwanni**). In contrast to the societies, the priesthoods are hereditary offices limited to a few persons. There are sixteen rain priesthoods, each one constituted by two to six members who have inherited their positions within matrilineal household groups. The power of the priests resides in the sacred fetish, one for each priesthood; these are the most sacred fetishes among the Zuni. The households keeping these fetishes are considered the most important families in the town. In the houses where the fetishes are kept their priests hold secret ceremonies for the supernatural rain makers, the *uwanammi*. The fetishes represent the *uwanammi*.

The main period to pray for rain and for ritual activities of the Rain Priests is the rainy season, the months July–September. Prayer sticks are planted at sacred springs, and thereafter the priests spend their time night and day for four days in their rooms, praying to the *uwanammi* and singing and fasting. One priesthood after another repeats the procedure. It is characteristic that the Rain Priests never engage in public ceremonies. Their main concern is the rain, and they promote its coming by quiet meditation. They are also doctors and diviners. The Rain Priests are expected to be peaceful and kind and have no quarrels with anybody. They are considered holy men and women. Formerly, they were not allowed to have any work to do other than that belonging to their sacerdotal duties. This is as close to a professional priesthood that one will see among Native Americans.

The Bow Priests (**apila ashiwanni**). This priesthood is associated with war and the *ahayuta*, the twin gods, warlike sons of the Sun, as we have seen mentioned in the Emergence Myth. The Bow Priests, recruited from warriors who have killed and scalped an enemy, were formerly war chiefs whose job it also was to protect the pueblo from witches. In earlier times a killer had to protect himself from the revenge of the ghost of his victim. He did that by becoming initiated into the Bow Priesthood at the same time that a scalp dance was conducted to propitiate the dangerous ghost.

Today there are only two Bow Priests left for obvious reasons: there are no more tribal wars, no scalping, and (officially at least) no witches. It was different in the old days, as recorded by Matilda Coxe Stevenson, when there was a chief priest and a battle chief and different functionaries for special tasks. Like other sacred organizations, the Bow Priests have a ceremonial chamber in a house in town where they keep their paraphernalia. Some of the fetishes they use are kept by officers outside their own ranks. The idols of the war twins, which figure in their ceremonies, have been carved by men of the Deer and Bear clans. These images play a role in the winter solstice ceremonies, the great annual occasion of the appearance of the Bow Priests. At that time new images are made of the twin gods, forming the center of a night of ceremonial singing. At dawn the following morning the idols are brought to two of the mountain shrines of the *ahayuta*. In the old days the Bow Priests held a great public dance after the harvest of the corn in the fall. As often has been the case in agricultural ceremonies around the world, the celebrations were accompanied by sexual license.

Besides these religious organizations, there have been other, smaller societies, which at the present time are mostly phenomena of the past. There is, however, one ceremonial figure who rises in power and sanctity above all others and that is *pekwin,* the priest of the Sun. The Sun, the father of all, is venerated at the midwinter and summer solstices on days decided upon by his priest. It seems that *pekwin's* observation of the rising and setting of the sun at certain landmarks helps this high priest determine the dates of these sacred periods. Another public ceremony, the Corn Dance each fourth summer, is also controlled by the *pekwin.* However, this ceremony is not primarily directed to the Sun, but to the departure and return of the Corn Maidens. Also other rituals are supervised by the priest of the Sun who is, in effect, the keeper of the calendar. He is also the chief of the other priests, officiating whenever the other priests come together. He installs the new priests and sanctions the impersonators of the *kachina* spirits. In addition he presides over the council of priests, six priests in all who have been the real political authority of the Zuni tribe.

However, the functions of the high priest are not carried out at present, because his position has been vacant since the 1940s. The ritual machinery moves on, but its main controller, the man who is responsible for the spiritual and material welfare of the Zuni, is gone. Perhaps this is convincing proof of the inherent strength in the ceremonial organization: it can run without its foremost director.

Altars, Masks, and Fetishes

The ceremonial system of the Zuni would be inexplicable without reference to the sacred objects handled by the organizations: the altars, masks, and fetishes. The altar is the focus of attention in ceremonies. It is placed in the room of ceremonies on the side away from the door and consists of fetishes and other sacred objects set on the floor in front of painted wooden slabs. This is the description of a Rain Society altar: eight corn-ear fetishes rest on a terrace design, from which lead eight discs of corn meal. These end up in two forks which are tipped with arrowheads. Along the discs there is a line of stone fetishes. Over the cloud terrace there are a number of arrowheads. Turtle shells surround the corn-ear fetishes. Four lines of corn meal form two crosses that are placed in a circle; as always in North America, such crosses placed within a circle are symbols of the world and the cardinal points.

As mentioned above, dancers and impersonators of gods turn

into these beings by donning masks. In fact, it is said that the *kachina* spirits, who are the chief "masked beings," at a certain time declined to visit human settlements in person, because on their return to the other world they "drew" the people along to their sacred lake. Instead, they told the Zuni to put on masks representing them and to perform the ceremonies they otherwise would have performed themselves. A mask is therefore naturally sacred and takes on the attributes of the god.

The representation of supernatural beings by masks is common in secret societies that have developed in horticultural settings. The mysterious experience of spirits received in visions has here been supplanted by the collective demonstration of spirits in dramatic performances, in which the presence of the spirit is expressed through the mask and skin of the spirit animal. There are certainly cases of visionary experiences among the Zuni, for example, as requirements for initiation into curing societies. (The shamanic background of the curing societies was pointed out above.) Moreover, the Rain Priests ingest a psychotropic drug, *Datura stramonium,* to become entranced and thus able to cure or perform divination. However, it is thought that the regular experience of the supernatural takes place in the ceremonies, not in visionary states. The masks are manifestations of the supernatural.

Masks are of many types. Half masks, or strips of leather worn over the face from the hairline to the mouth and from ear to ear, are often worn by female deities. Complete face masks have molded nose and lips and eye holes but are not realistically formed; rather the faces are exaggerated into caricatures. Helmet masks encircle the head like a rounded bag over the top of the head. These masks, which completely cover the dancer's head, are made of deer or buffalo skin or simply cowhide. The mask is usually crowned by bunches of feathers; the more feathers, the more important is the *kachina.* Downy feathers represent "the breath of the rain." Realistic symbols like attached deer horns or stylized geometric symbols indicate possible supernatural associations. In addition, masks are painted with the same designs as those we find on ceremonial pottery, altar boards, and sand paintings, a testimony of strong religious integration. The masks generally display a fine degree of craftsmanship.

There are more than a hundred types of masks, each one having a particular name and portraying a particular god or spirit. All may be classified into two general divisions. One division comprises very ancient masks that remain tribal property. They represent high-ranking *kachina* gods and are considered most dangerous. They are kept in sealed jars in houses, and their hereditary guardians are the owners of these houses. Such masks demand food sacrifices in the river to the ancestors before anyone can wear them and the planting of prayer sticks and four days of sexual continence after wearing. The other main category is masks that are individual property. Such a mask serves as a person's personal fetish. Some have several such masks. After an individual's death the mask is buried at the *kachina* village to maintain that person's status among the *kachinas* just joined. Only the departed who have such masks may return in spirit to visit the Zuni in *kachina* dances.

We come finally to all the talismans, stones, feathers, ears of corn, and other objects scholars include under the general term "fetishes." "Fetish" was originally a term that the Portuguese applied to the sacred objects of West Africa. However, it has been commonly used about Zuni sacred objects since Frank Cushing wrote his classic (but confused) study, *Zuñi Fetiches* (1883). These fetishes—which also include masks—do not stand isolated from other American Indian cultic phenomena. Just as the Zuni masked beings in ritual processions are substitutes for the visionary spirits in the rest of North America, so the different sorts of Zuni fetishes supplant the medicine bags found elsewhere. Their functions are the same: both the fetish and the medicine bag are visible signs of the bonds between the supernatural order and humans. The fetish is itself powerful: if neglected or desecrated it may strike its keeper with misfortune.

No Pueblo Indians make such extensive use of ceremonialism as the Zuni, and no Pueblo Indians have paid such great attention to fetishes as the Zuni. Everyone may have a personal fetish, such as a little stone found in the mountains, which, due to its peculiar form or color, is thought to have supernatural properties. Such smaller fetishes are usually the individual's hunting charms and are kept in buckskin bags hanging around the owner's neck when hunting. They are the most common fetishes and help people catch and slay wild game. A relic of the old animal ceremonialism is the idea that by proper use of the fetish the spirit of the slain animal attains life after death.

The more powerful fetishes are not individual property but associated with the ceremonial societies, particularly with the priests. The fetishes of the Rain Priests, the **ettowe**, are the most sancrosanct objects in Zuni and the source of power of the priests. They are of two kinds, water fetishes and corn fetishes. They are said to be petrified supernatural beings. According to tradition they were carried by the first ancestors from the fourth underworld and are now preserved in sealed pottery jars in the same houses where they have been since Emergence days. The medicine societies have in their custody large animallike fetishes, such as stone images of the beast gods. They decorate the painted slab altars of these societies. Each image is fed regularly at mealtime every day by some woman living in the house where it is kept. There is a hole one to four inches in diameter in one side of the jar, and through this hole the fetish is fed.

The fetishes that often vaguely resemble animals are used in a most concrete way in curative rites. For instance, the Ant Society cures skin diseases by placing its fetish, an effigy of a red ant tied to a horn medicine pouch, on the patient's pillow near the face. The red ant takes the disease away through the sick person's mouth. The procedure is accompanied by chanting each morning for twelve days by the society members.

Offerings

The feeding of fetishes is of course not the only form of offerings in Zuni religion. Other supernaturals who receive food offerings are the ancestors. Before a meal everyone participating in it selects a bit of each food dish, breathes on it, and says, "Receive! (Oh, souls of) my ancestry, and eat; resuscitate by means of your wondrous knowledge, your hearts; return unto us of yours the water we need, of yours the seeds of earth, of yours the means of attaining great age." When this grace has been said the selected food is cast into the fire. Frank Cushing, who in the nineteenth century reported this prayer, added that he had never seen a Zuni, young or old, taste food without first giving this invocation, although sometimes in abbreviated form.[43] There is one great offering day to the ancestors, Grandmothers' Day (the same as All Souls Day), when great quantities of food are sacrificed in the river or in the fire. Catholic and indigenous religious practices have merged in this rite.

Offerings of food are made regularly to ancestors, *kachinas*, and fetishes. Another type of offering consists of prayer meal, that is, corn meal mixed with ground white shells and turquoise. This meal is offered to the Sun each morning and sprinkled as a sanctifying element on sacred objects and *kachina* dancers. It is also used to delineate sacred paths, and it is rubbed on the newborn and the dead.

Prayer sticks are also a kind of offering. They usually consist of red willow staffs to which feathers are attached; they are painted with symbolic colors (for instance, blue and yellow for fecundity). They are planted in corn fields, springs, and mountain shrines, and followed by restrictions on sexual intercourse and food for the one who plants them. Prayer sticks communicate a prayer and are accompanied by oral prayers. As Bunzel has noted, prayers constitute the heart of each ceremony, and are—like fetishes—sacred and powerful in themselves. Prayers are directed to the supernaturals, who are the controllers of the universe.

The offerings can be understood partly as gifts to the supernaturals, in particular the food offerings, but most of all they express the sentiment of communion with the supernatural powers. However, prayer meal and prayer sticks are primarily expressions of a feeling of the balance within life: the balance between humans and the supernatural as well as the balance within all ingredients in an ordered universe. It is people's task to contribute to this cosmic balance through personal behavior and through participation in the necessary rituals. Prayer meal and prayer sticks are parts of these rituals and a personal means of promoting the individual and collective welfare that is an integral part of the all-pervasive cosmic balance.

The Ritual Year

There has been much talk here of ritual performances, and little demonstration of them. The reasons are obvious. The rituals are so many, so diversified, and so rich that it would be an impossible task to present them in this short survey. After all, each society—and as we have seen there are many societies—has its own set of rituals in the annual round. We will have to be satisfied here with a general account of the ceremonial round, in which the main ritual procedures and the major appearances of the ritual organizations will be mentioned, and a closer view of one of these organizations, the most renowned and popular of them all, the *kachina* dancers.

A preliminary presentation of the calendar year in its basic outline and meaning has already been given. As is so common in American Indian ceremonialism, the ritual year has a double reference: it relates to cosmic events, the harmony between spirits and humans, and also to the changes of the seasons that have meaning for human subsistence. In an agricultural setting it is the vegetative year that is important. Changes in plant life are marked with ritual measures and the appearances of ceremonial organizations. Among the Zuni these interrelationships are extremely complicated and not known in every detail; or the details vary according to the accounts of field investigators.[44]

As pointed out, the ritual year is divided into two halves separated by the winter and summer solstices. The winter and spring ceremonies are concerned with medicine, war, and fertility; the summer and fall ceremonies with rain and crops. The exact time of the winter solstice (the month of "Turning Back," that is, of the sun) is determined by the priest of the Sun, *pekwin,* who, from a cornfield east of the town, observes the time when the sun rises over a certain point of Corn Mountain. The celebrations are introduced by a period of ceremonial constraint indicating the critical juncture between the old year and the new: no fire must be seen, animal food must be avoided, trading is forbidden, and sexual continence has to be observed. However, in one of the *kivas* a sacred fire is kept burning. If these regulations should be disregarded, the safe transition of the world from one period to another might be endangered.

This is therefore a period of intense ritual activity. Thus, the medicine societies have their nightly retreats, followed by the planting of prayer sticks to the beast gods and the *kachinas*. The priests, in their retreats, pray for rain and fertility and then deposit prayer sticks at springs. Each family sets out ears of corn, rain fetishes, and personal fetishes at night, praying for good crops, flocks of sheep, and the fecundity of women.

On the twentieth day of these celebrations the new year is brought from the east by two masked gods. They arrive at the chief *kiva* and dance together with the priests assembled there all through the night. The old year is "sent out," and a new fire is kindled in the morning. All over the town of Zuni, people enjoy the occasion and come to fetch live coals from this fire, returning with the coals to light their home fires. Many people go to the main *kiva* to be blessed by the masked gods, and all rejoice and dance until sundown.

There is now a cleaning of the previous year's refuse from the houses, a ritual procedure that is coupled to the fate of the corn. The man of each household takes out the accumulated refuse and stacks it on the ground as if it were corn: the refuse represents the corn. Similarly, the woman carries out the ashes and sprinkles them as she would sprinkle corn meal at the harvest. Everybody, indeed, sprinkles corn meal and prays to the Sun. Omens of a good or bad harvest are studied. Houses are symbolically cleansed from witchcraft. At the same time, the men who have been chosen to impersonate the *kachina* gods appearing at the end of the year, the Shalako ceremony, are summoned by the Bow Priests to start their ritual training. This training will continue throughout the year, always in the evenings.

After the midwinter rites have ended the *kachina* dancers begin their season of public dances, which lasts from February to September. This is also the season of the growth of the corn, which is stimulated by these dances. The ears of corn exposed at the midwinter celebrations are planted in March. The planting must always be carried out ceremonially in holes representing the six directions. The planter sprinkles a cross of meal and places a prayer stick at its intersection, all the time chanting sacred songs. Then he fasts for four days.

The midsummer is spent planting prayer sticks, making offerings, and saying prayers to the rain makers. Impersonators of the *kachina* clowns, the **koyemshi,** visit all houses and are doused with water by the women—a symbolic reference to the need to water the corn plants. A few days later the summer rain dances start, to promote the coming of the rains. At this time every fourth year there is a pilgrimage to Kachina Village, the lake about eighty miles west of Zuni. A deputation of *kachina* dancers offers prayer sticks at the shrines there.

As the first ears ripen in August they are brought home and put together with a perfect ear, the "corn father," and a double ear, the "corn mother," both taken from the granary. This green corn ritual refers to the return of the Corn Maidens, according to the myth.

November is general harvest time. The woman of the house lays the finest ears of new corn aside, greets them in a ceremonial way and sprinkles them with flowers, pollen, and water. She preserves them in a pouch, bringing them out again at midwinter and at spring planting next year. This feast is accompanied ·by sexual license, which in all fertility religions is part of the ritual reproduction process.

The year ends with the coming of the *shalako* at the end of November, possibly the greatest ceremony in aboriginal North America. The *shalako* are the messengers of the rain gods (the dead) and probably, as Parsons thought, spirits of the deer; the six gigantic masked figures that represent them symbolize the six directions and the deer. They make an enormous impression. The dancers impersonating them carry a ten-foot-long pole in their hands that holds up the costume and has the facial mask on the top. The dancer has to look out through a hole in the blanket covering the "upper body."

These supernatural beings come from the desert bringing blessings of fertility and long life. Their arrival is a great occasion. In the words of a well-initiated Zuni to that famous pioneer ethnographer Frank Cushing: "Little brother, make your heart glad—a great festival is now everyone's thought. Eighteen days more, and from the west will come the *sha-la-k'o;* it welcomes the return of the *Ka-ka* [kachinas] and speeds the departure of the Sun."[45] What has been called "the coming of the gods" is a public festival of fourteen days' duration in the late part of November or early part of December.[46] Preceded by the *koyemshi* clowns and accompanied by singers, the giant figures approach the town and halt on the south bank of the Zuni River. Ruth Bunzel has ably described her impression of the coming of the gods: "As soon as it is quite dark the six Ca'lako [*shalako*] cross the river quietly and then suddenly rise out of the river bed, each surrounded by a group of singers from his *kiva,* all singing antiphonal songs. This is the most impressive moment in the Ca'lako [*shalako*] ceremonies. The songs are magnificent, and the sudden appearance of the six giant figures in the moonlight is superb." Thereafter the masked beings go to their respective houses where they spend the night dancing. The peculiar figure "fills the room, from floor to ceiling, and its crest of eagle feathers brushes the beams. Dancing in the house they [the impersonators] resemble nothing so much as animated gargoyles with their huge heads and tiny legs and their clattering beaks. They bend over and clap their beaks in the face of anyone who dozes in the house."[47]

During these festivals, which are open to the public, even white visitors, there are prayers for fertility, corn growth, and health. As one informant told Bunzel, "When Ca'lako [*shalako*] comes he brings in all different kinds of seeds, wild things, and peaches and pumpkins and beans and corn. Then when spring comes, the man who has had Ca'lako [*shalako*] house plants these seeds in his fields."[48] When the *shalako* leave for the west again the dances continue for some time, and everybody is happy. That ends the year.

Kachina Dancers

Next we turn to the ritual organization to which the *shalako* dancers may be counted, the *kachina* dancers. As mentioned in the foregoing, the *kachinas,* or *koko,* are spirits of the first ancestors, the dead, the clouds and rains who live in the sacred lake or the clouds who live up on the mountains. They are the masked gods, that is, they are primarily known through the performances of the masked Zuni dancers who represent them. The *kachina* cult is, as Ruth Bunzel says, the dominant Zuni cult, both because of its spectacular ceremonies and because of its support by all males; no man refrains from playing an active role in the organization if he wants to be certain of living on after death. The ritual contribution that a man can make in the *kachina* ceremonies and that lasts at least until he is in later middle age is necessary work to align the Zuni with the cosmic forces that keep everything, including their very existence, alive. The *kachina* organization membership is more than a social duty, it is a religious necessity. We are indeed far from the individualism of Shoshoni religion!

One could certainly account for the attraction of the *kachina* cult also in other terms, for example, its beauty and gaiety. This and the friendliness and easy ways of the *kachina* spirits are qualities that have no doubt endeared them and their pageants to the Zuni people. And yet, it is a fact that the *kachina* spirits severely punish any impersonator who does not represent them correctly: the mask might choke him. Persons appearing in *kachina* apparel, in turn, demand respect from the onlookers, for they are the gods as soon as they have put on the masks. Besides the masks, which as fetishes have been described in the foregoing, *kachina* dancers wear costumes, in particular white cotton kilts, sashes, and high buckskin moccasins. They carry gourd rattles or bow and arrows or feather staves, depending on their roles.

Some *kachina* figures are very sacred and have individual names. These are the **kachina priests**, the priestly hierarchy that rules the Kachina Village in the beyond. There is for instance the chief of these *kachinas*, **Pautiwa**. He is impersonated by a member of one particular clan who is venerably treated in connection with his appearance at the New Year ceremonies. Another important figure is **Long Horn** who sends the deer—apparently an old supernatural master of the animals. Impersonators of the *shalako* form a cult group for the time they serve, as do the impersonators of the *koyemshi* ("mudheads"), clown *kachinas*. At the New Year celebrations the priests appoint a leader of the clowns, Father Koyemshi, who in his turn appoints nine other clowns. They all serve for four years, entertaining between rain dances with comic and obscene performances. The Shalako festival, for instance, is introduced by "pornographic" appearances of the sacred clowns.

The sacred clowns, whose buffooneries amuse small children as well as adults, represent on a ritual level the trickster personage in mythology. (Stories about the trickster Coyote are found also among the Zuni.) The clowns disrupt the ceremonial stress, release tensions, and make ceremonies endurable. Generally in North American ceremonialism, mirth and sacred gravity exist side by side, and this is the case with the Zuni. However, the *koyemshi* are dangerous—whoever touches them becomes crazy. The Zuni never forget the supernatural, irrational character of the beings they impersonate.

The *kachina* dancers appear in two series of performances, the winter dances after the midwinter solstice held in the *kivas* and the summer dances (rain dances) held on the open plaza in the town. They also participate as assistant dancers when other societies and priesthoods have their ritual performances. They are indeed the backbone of Zuni ceremonialism, supposed to bring health, rain, and fertility in their masked appearances. This is an extract of the prayer a Shalako *kachina* recites when he enters a Zuni house in early December:

I have come from the sacred lake and I have come by all the springs.
. . . I have come to see my people. For many years I have heard of my
people living here at Itiwana [the middle of the world] and for long I
have wanted to come. I want them to be happy, and I have been praying for them; and especially I want the women to be fortunate with
their babies. I bring my people all kinds of seeds, all the different
kinds of corn and all different kinds of fruit and wild green things. I
have been praying for my people to have long life; and whoever has an
evil heart should stand up in the daylight. I have been praying that
my people may have all different kinds of seeds and that their rooms
may be full of corn of all colors and beans of all colors and pumpkins
and water gourds, and that they may have plenty of fresh water, so
that they may look well and be healthy because of the pumpkins and
the beans and the corn. I want to see them healthy.[49]

This is the kind of prayer found among all North American Indians, although in this case it is the *shalako* or divine protectors, once
living members of the Zuni tribe, who offer the prayer. Life, securi-
ty, food, and drink—these are the gifts for people if they comply
with the ritual and metaphysical order. Indeed, the concept of harmony with the supernatural order brings to the fore parallels in other religions—for instance, Vedic *rita* and Chinese *tao*. The wealth
and beauty of Zuni rituals to adapt humans and their society to the
cosmic harmony is well known and surpasses everything we know in
North American ceremonialism.

Zuni Religion Today

No religion that is so intimately connected with culture and society
as Zuni religion can in the long run withstand the change of time,
especially when the presuppositions of this culture become altered.
This is what is happening in our day. The new type of tribal government today is reducing the importance of sacral leaders. The pressure from a new social style and way of life makes itself felt. There is
also a transition from horticulture to new ways of living such as
working for money (employment among the whites), trade, and
commercialism (for instance, in the distribution of Zuni art objects).

As could be expected, religion, although conservative, slowly follows suit and also changes.

Old myths have disappeared, and many old ideas and rituals have become forgotten. On the other hand, some spectacular rituals have become more elaborate. Thus, the *kachina* cult has become more important in this century than it ever was before. Its elaboration is certainly associated with the decline of priesthoods and secret societies. The latter do not seem to respond to the demands of a changing life-style. The war priests, for example, also called Bow Priests, cannot function meaningfully now after the end of tribal wars. Some Zuni have been involved in the global wars of the last fifty years, but they are reluctant to equate modern warfare with ancient Zuni war practice. The result has been that there is no natural recruitment to the Bow Priesthood any more. The same applies to the other organizations: it is difficult to find people who are interested in practicing old-fashioned medicine or invoking the rain.

Just as among the Plains Indians the old religion has become concentrated in the Sun Dance ceremony, so with the Zuni Indians religion is increasingly receiving its main support from *kachina* ceremonies. It is difficult to know if in the long run this development will overthrow the structure of the Zuni religious system, but it will certainly modify the picture that we have presented here. Until now this system has been sufficiently closed to exclude many new Indian religious currents, such as the peyote religion, which is so important for contemporary Shoshoni. The individualistic character of Peyotism and its socially disruptive emphasis on personal experiences are not at all in line with the spirit of Zuni religion. The same is true for other Pueblo groups, except for the Plains-influenced Taos among whom use of peyote has been allowed, although not fully accepted.

The role of the Catholic church is an interesting chapter in Zuni religious development. There are church buildings both in Zuni itself and in the surrounding area, and the Catholic fathers certainly have Zuni in attendance at their services. However, the Zuni circumstances are not favorable to Catholicism on a more genuine level. Cushing has called attention to the nature of aboriginal reactions to the Catholic mission. When in the 1770s the Church of Our Lady of Guadalupe was built, Zuni artists painted the walls with traditional symbols of the gods of wind, rain, lightning, sunlight, tempest, and war and with emblems of the Corn Maidens amidst

Christian decorations. The Catholic fathers did not realize the nature of this symbolism but were happy to see the zeal of the native painters in working, as they thought, for Catholicism. From then on, the Indians were eager to attend mass, to be baptized, and have their names written in the baptismal registers—"names totemic of the sacred assemblies"—which were thus legitimized by the church representatives who did not understand their meanings. As Cushing says, the Indians did not even think of renouncing their allegiance to Zuni gods. Rather, the Zuni wanted to gain the force of purification and the name-potency of the God and spirits (angels, saints) of another people and at the same time to assure the recognition of their own gods and priests by the foreign gods and priests. Indeed, tribal medicine feathers and fetishes were hidden under the altar of the church.[50]

Such incidents have set the pattern for today's devotion to Catholicism. Catholic sacred beings and symbols are incorporated into Zuni religion insofar as they comply with the traditional pattern, and Catholic attendance is largely seen in the perspective of traditional religion. For instance, among the Zuni fetishes there is a Catholic *santo* (saint) that people took care of when an old mission was abandoned in the beginning of the last century. The image, twelve inches tall, portrays the Christ Child of Our Lady of Atocha. It is kept in a shrine under the Shalako ceiling altar. The shrine is crowned by a cross. The image, whose garments are adorned by votive offerings, is fed daily like other fetishes. According to the Zuni, the Christ Child was borne by a daughter of the Sun. There is a dance each fall for the *santo* who is supposed to bring fertility for humans, animals, and fields.[51]

It has been argued by some researchers that the *kachina* cult has been inspired by the Catholic veneration of saints. This argument could be accepted if we keep in mind that the *kachina* cult as such originated in pre-Christian times and later received a veneer of Catholicism. A closer investigation of Zuni religious and ceremonial forms might reveal many influences of this kind.

The mixture of Zuni traditional practices with Catholicism is no sign of deterioration of the Pueblo religious pattern, but rather of change and, in some respects, of enrichment. However, in a larger perspective, the change in the conditions of living and the impact of Western value standards may threaten the future of Zuni traditional religion.

CHAPTER V

Conclusion: Unity and Diversity in Native American Religions

The sketches of two North American Indian religions offer us examples of two ways in which humans have tried to solve the eternal question of the nature of reality and how people relate to that reality. "Religion" is the name usually given to the cultural constructions founded on this basic and yet quite complex human concern.[52] Of course ecology, society, and historical traditions contribute to the final shape of such religious forms. However, what is most important is the identification of a religious reality that goes beyond all natural, social, and historical conditions.

The earliest tribes who long ago took possession of North America were the bearers of a hunting culture and a hunter's outlook on the supernatural world. We have seen how elements of this hunting ideology are preserved in the traditions of all later Indian groups, even among such an agricultural tribe as the Zuni. However, as cultures became differentiated and particularly with the rise of agriculture, new religious forms arose that corresponded more closely to the conditions of the new cultural patterns. There is no doubt that at present, facing integration with white material (and also social) culture, Indian religions are again on the verge of dramatic changes; older Native American forms that are no longer relevant will be threatened and may disappear, but Native American religions will not give way completely to Western religious (and areligious) values.

Wind River Shoshoni and Zuni religions demonstrate the great

128

diversity of Native American traditions within very different ecological, social, and historical conditions. As was mentioned in the first chapter, there is no single "American Indian religion" that is uniform throughout North America (or North and South America). In general, there are two basic religious orientations found in North America, a hunting pattern (as seen among the Shoshoni) and a horticultural pattern (as among the Zuni). Each of these particular traditions has retained its distinctive religious heritage, while changing so that it is in tune with the historical and social context.

The Wind River Shoshoni have remained strong individualists long after the end of their hunting days on the open Plains and in the Rocky Mountain forests. The infusion of Plains culture from the east modified their cultural and social individualism: they became devoted to the more collective activities of the Sun Dance and military drill but in other aspects continued to be "wild and disorganized like birds," as one observer has put it. Their guardian spirit complex expresses the Shoshoni individual quest for supernatural help and protection in hunting, warfare, and other pursuits. On the other hand, the Sun Dance ceremony is a collective ritual of thanksgiving and petition for the success and well-being of the whole tribe from one summer to the next. In extraordinary situations, such as sickness, when the individual's religious and secular resources are of no avail, medicine men come to the rescue of the individual.

As is typical of hunting religions, Shoshoni religion features a rather loose integration of religion, society, and culture. The individual is emphasized at the expense of society and culture. This relative lack of integration is demonstrated in the tension between mythology and cult, with mutually exclusive ideological patterns. The tales of mythology have very little to do with everyday ritual, and rituals such as the Sun Dance have very little connection with mythology. Another example of the loose integration of Shoshoni religion is the high degree of diversity of religious concepts from individual to individual; within the boundaries of the religious pattern, ideas are flexible and shift considerably.

Because religious ideas are so flexible and the organization of the worldview is so loose, a number of belief complexes are formed that pull together and unify otherwise separate beliefs and practices. For example, individual beliefs form links, like links of a chain, and these connect an association of beliefs into a larger complex. This is seen in the interconnection of guardian spirits with the medicine man's spiritualism as well as with the diagnosis and cure of disease and ideas about the spirits of the dead. Each link can be seen as an individual belief when viewed separately, but in the actual practice of Shoshoni religion, these links become forged together into a unified "complex" of related beliefs and ritual action. Such links, as individual elements, may be at variance or even in apparent conflict with one another, but they become coordinated and unified within the religious complex. Shoshoni religion, which features both a loose social organization and a flexible set of ideas or "philosophy," tends to encourage the unification of individual elements as complexes. The general organization and philosophy within Shoshoni religion varies considerably from individual to individual, and is guided by personal religious experience such as dreams and visions.

The Zuni show a reverse picture, suppressing rather than emphasizing the individual and experiential side of religion. Some scholars such as Ruth Benedict may have exaggerated the Zuni preference for the collective tradition, but it does contrast sharply with the Shoshoni. And when viewed in terms of Native American religions in general, the Zuni represent the horticultural pattern of religious orientation and emphasize the collectivism and cooperation essential in an agricultural society with greater population density.

The Zuni form one of the clearest cases of the horticultural pattern: their socioreligious organization is unsurpassed in complexity throughout North America. One probable historical reason for this complexity is that the organizations and functions in the ancient "seven cities of Cibola," as the Spaniards called the Zuni pueblos, came to be concentrated in one settlement after the Pueblo revolt in the 1680s. The ceremonial system was contracted and therefore became more complex with, as Parsons describes it, "reduplication or elaboration of ceremonials." In earlier times there was exclusive association of the Shalako ceremony with the ancient pueblo of Hawikuh. In modern days, there is overlapping of the functions of *pekwin* with those of the town chief. The concentration of Zuni religion resulted in an enormous machinery, an intertwined web of religious activities, social roles, and cultural objectives. Ruth Bunzel has remarked that, although religion pervades all activities and the Zuni are one of the most religious peoples of the world, "in all the enormous mass of rituals there is no single bit of religious feeling equal in intensity and exaltation to the usual vision quest of the North American Indian." Bunzel considers that among the Zuni, religion has been externalized in rituals instead of internalized in religious feelings.[53] Perhaps this is true in a generalized sense, but we can scarcely rule out the occurrence of individual piety.

Behind the elaborateness of Zuni ritual there is a unitary religious conviction that the world order is founded on a balance of interrelationships between humankind, the universe, and the supernatural powers. The ritual organization and processes are directed to conform to this conception of world harmony. The rituals operate together with, and thereby strengthen, the well-being of the pueblo. To call this system magic is to depreciate the nature of the convictions involved.

Bunzel has claimed that there is a lack of profounder cosmological thought and metaphysics in Zuni mythology. If so, there is a change from the days when Cushing recorded the origin tales. The inference of the Zuni ritual symbolism is clear: the cosmos is a harmonious whole or spiritual order that also includes humankind. There is no explicit statement in so many words of this thought—no prophets, no authoritative philosophers—but it illuminates the structure of Zuni religion.

The Shoshoni and Zuni represent the unity as well as the diversity of Native American religions. The Shoshoni and Zuni, like other American Indians, share many features such as a notion of affinity to plants, animals, and all of nature. The Shoshoni emphasize their relationship to animals; the Zuni retain some of the old animal ceremonialism but focus primarily on their relationship to maize. Shoshoni view the universe in the four sacred (cardinal) directions, while Zuni expand the four sacred directions to six—to include zenith and nadir.

All Native Americans look to "natural spirits" or the spirits of nature for revelation and power, and this is true of Shoshoni and Zuni. However, Shoshoni look more to animals and the sky, whereas Zuni look to plants and the underground. Religious architecture mirrors both their understanding of the universe and the two diverse forms of expression. For the Shoshoni the cosmos is reconstructed in the Sun Dance lodge, open to the sun and the elements, built on any site. For the Zuni, the cosmos and its "emergence" is reflected in the permanent *kiva,* with its *sipapu* or ceremonial hole of emergence; for rituals the Zuni "descend" into the *kiva.*

The Shoshoni recognize Mother Earth, but they focus mainly on the power in the sky; the Zuni recognize the preeminence of the Sun, but their main concern is with the sacredness of the wombs of the world and the underground. The supernatural reveals its power to American Indians: to Shoshoni, the power comes mainly to individuals in dreams and visions; to Zuni, the power is conveyed especially to groups in the myth of origin and in collective annual rituals.

Shoshoni and Zuni religions express two distinctive approaches to the mystery and sacredness of life, both stamped by their Indian heritage, but communicating the Indian conviction of religious reality to the rest of the world.

Notes

1. Further discussion of this circumpolar heritage can be found in my article "North American Indian Religions in a Circumpolar Perspective," *North American Indian Studies: European Contributions,* ed. Pieter Hovens (Göttingen: Edition Herodot, 1981), pp. 11–28.

2. A. Irving Hallowell, "Bear Ceremonialism in the Northern Hemisphere," *American Anthropologist* 28, no. 1 (1926): 1–175.

3. The trickster has been discussed from a humanistic perspective in Paul Radin, *The Trickster: A Study in American Indian Mythology* (New York: Philosophical Library, 1956); and from the perspective of comparative religion in my book, *The Religions of the American Indians* (Berkeley and Los Angeles: University of California Press, 1979), pp. 29–43.

4. Robert Redfield, *The Primitive World and Its Transformations* (Ithaca, N.Y.: Cornell University Press, 1953), p. 85.

5. Åke Hultkrantz, *Belief and Worship in Native North America,* ed. Christopher Vecsey (Syracuse, N.Y.: Syracuse University Press, 1981), pp. 117–34.

6. Frank G. Speck, *Nasukapi: The Savage Hunters of the Labrador Peninsula* (Norman, Okla.: University of Oklahoma Press, 1935), pp. 33f.

7. Alfonso Ortiz, *The Tewa World: Space, Time, Being and Becoming in a Pueblo Society* (Chicago: University of Chicago Press, 1969).

8. Ibid., p. 98.

9. Edna Kenton, ed., *The Jesuit Relations and Allied Documents* (New York: Vanguard Press, 1954), pp. 113, 141f.

10. James R. Walker, "The Sun Dance and Other Ceremonies of the Oglala Division of the Teton Dakota," *Anthropological Papers of the American Museum of Natural History* 16, no. 2 (New York, 1917): 157, 160. Cf. the interpretation in Werner Müller, *Amerika: Die Neue oder die Alte Welt?* (Berlin: Dietrich Reimer, 1982), pp. 36–51.

11. Paul Radin, *Primitive Religion* (New York: Dover Publications, 1957): 3–4.

12. Cf. my article, "Accommodation and Persistence: Ecological Analysis of the Religion of the Sheepeater Indians in Wyoming, U.S.A.," *Temenos* 17 (1981): 35–44.

13. See my *Belief and Worship*, pp. 28–47, and my article, "An Ideological Dichotomy: Myths and Folk Beliefs Among the Shoshoni," in *Sacred Narrative: Readings in the Theory of Myth*, ed. Alan Dundes (Berkeley and Los Angeles: University of California Press, 1984), pp. 152–65.

14. See my *Belief and Worship*, pp. 157–84.

15. See my article, "The Concept of the Soul Held by the Wind River Shoshone," *Ethnos* 16, nos. 1–2 (Stockholm 1951): 18–44.

16. Instead of the supernatural owner of the animals the *puha* animal is supposed to control the animals. For an analysis of these problems among the Shoshoni, see my article, "The Master of the Animals among the Wind River Shoshoni," *Ethnos* 26, no. 4 (1961): 198–218.

17. Arnold van Gennep, *The Rites of Passage* (Chicago: University of Chicago Press, 1960).

18. There is no similar exact time for the boys' ceremonies. For customs at menstruation and childbirth, see also Demitri B. Shimkin, "Childhood and Development among the Wind River Shoshone," *Anthropological Records* 5, no. 5 (Berkeley and Los Angeles: University of California Press, 1947).

19. This holistic interpretation of couvade is preferable to the efforts made by some social anthropologists to regard it as a way of asserting the father's paternity, or as a means to save the wife from evil spirits and transfer the latter on her husband.

20. Demitri B. Shimkin, "The Wind River Shoshone Sun Dance," *Bureau of American Ethnology*, Bulletin 151 (Washington 1953): 409ff.; Åke Hultkrantz, "Yellow Hand, Chief and Medicine-man among the Eastern Shoshoni," *Proceedings of the 38th Congress of Americanists* (Stuttgart and München 1968): 293–304.

21. This is one of the few visions where there is reference to Our Father. One of my informants even thought that it was Our Father himself who appeared in this vision.

22. The emphasis on curing is most certainly a reflection of the changed aims of the ceremony introduced about 1890.

23. This is of course an instance of animal ceremonialism.

24. A more exhaustive presentation will be found in my *Belief and Worship,* pp. 235–263.

25. Cf. Hultkrantz, *Iconography of Religions: Prairie and Plains Indians* (Leiden: Brill, 1973), pp. 9–18.

26. See my *Belief and Worship,* pp. 212–34.

27. Ibid., pp. 264–81.

28. Zuni—sometimes spelled Zuñi, but nowadays not pronounced that way—is a Keresan name of the pueblo. The Zuni themselves call their town Ashiwi. The Spaniards of the sixteenth century called the pueblos "los siete ciudades de Cibola," the seven towns of Cibola.

29. Alfred L. Kroeber, "Zuñi," *Encyclopaedia of Religion and Ethics,* ed. James Hastings (New York: Scribner, 1928), 12:868–73.

30. Fred Eggan, *Social Organization of the Western Pueblos* (Chicago: University of Chicago Press, 1950), pp. 210–222.

31. Frank Cushing, "Outlines of Zuñi Creation Myths," 13th *Annual Report of the Bureau of Ethnology* (Washington 1896): 379–81. On the world-parents myth, see Anna Birgitta Rooth, "The Creation Myths of the North American Indians," in *Sacred Narrative: Readings in the Theory of Myth,* ed. Alan Dundes (Berkeley and Los Angeles: University of California Press, 1984), pp. 171–73.

32. Elsie Clews Parsons, "The Origin Myth of Zuñi," *Journal of American Folk-Lore,* vol. 36 (1923): 135–62. A. L. Kroeber, "Zuñi," p. 869. Frank H. Cushing, "Outlines of Zuñi Creation Myths." *Thirteenth Annual Report of the Bureau of Ethnology.* Washington, 1896: 379–447.

33. Cf. Ruth Benedict, *Zuni Mythology* (New York: Columbia University Press, 1935), 1:256.

34. The universe is thus basically restricted to this landscape. A Hopi friend of mine told me of the shock he experienced when for the first time he saw the Pacific Ocean from the California coast.

35. Those who have studied the recent works of Claude Lévi-Strauss should know that in his book series *Mythologiques* he treats lengthily the distinction between "raw" and "cooked." His argument does not, however, concern us here.

36. See for instance plates X and XI in Frank H. Cushing, "Zuñi Fetiches," 2nd *Annual Report of the Bureau of Ethnology* (Washington 1883). The same "lifelines" are found on Zuni pottery.

37. Ruth L. Bunzel, "Introduction to Zuñi Ceremonialism," 47th *Annual Report of the Bureau of American Ethnology* (Washington 1932): 483f.

38. Benedict, *Zuni Mythology,* vol. 1, pp. 20–43, 269–272.

39. Ruth L. Bunzel, "Zuñi Ritual Poetry," 47th *Annual Report of the Bureau of American Ethnology* (Washington 1932): 804.

40. See Herman Karl Haeberlin, "The Idea of Fertilization in the Culture of the Pueblo Indians," *Memoirs of the American Anthropological Association* 3, no. 1 (Lancaster 1916). Cf. also Hultkrantz, *Belief and Worship,* pp. 107–11.

41. Quoted after Benedict, *Zuni Mythology,* vol. 2, pp. 128–134. In a version given by Cushing the wife is recovered from the Kachina Village by Owls who instruct the man to observe continence on the way back to Zuni. However, he breaks the taboo, and his wife becomes an owl. From this event dates the mourning for the dead: Frank H. Cushing, *Zuñi Folk Tales* (New York: Knopf, 1931), pp. 18–32.

42. Bunzel, "Introduction to Zuñi Ceremonialism," p. 476.

43. Frank H. Cushing, *Zuñi: Selected Writings,* ed. by Jesse Green (Lincoln, Nebr.: University of Nebraska Press, 1979), pp. 306f.

44. To the following, see Elsie Clews Parsons, *Pueblo Indian Religion* (Chicago: University of Chicago Press, 1939), vol. 1, pp. 514–531, vol. 2, pp. 791–793; Parsons, "Notes on Zuñi, Part I," *Memoirs of the American Anthropological Association* IV, no. 3 (Lancaster, Pa., 1917); and Bunzel, "Introduction to Zuñi Ceremonialism," pp. 534–540.

45. Cushing, *Zuñi: Selected Writings,* pp. 75f.

46. For the festivals, see Ruth L. Bunzel, "Zuñi Katcinas," 47th *Annual Report of the Bureau of American Ethnology* (Washington 1932): 941–975.

47. Bunzel, "Zuñi Katcinas," p. 973.

48. Ibid., p. 975.

49. Ibid., p. 974.

50. Cushing, *Zuñi: Selected Writings,* pp. 176–178.

51. Ruth F. Kirk, "Introduction to Zuni Fetishism," *Papers of the School of American Research* (Sante Fe 1943): 16f.

52. Cf. my article, "The Concept of the Supernatural in Primal Religion," *History of Religions* 22, no. 3 (1983): 231–253.

53. Bunzel, "Introduction to Zuñi Ceremonialism," p. 480.

Glossary

ahayuta. The diminutive twin war gods of the Zuni.

animal ceremonialism. The rituals around the slain game, in particular the disposal of the carcass whereby the bones are laid in their anatomical order and the head is sometimes elevated on a tree or a pole. The ceremonialism is intended to propitiate the animal or its spiritual master who is supposed to have been offended by the killing. The order of the bones is an objectivation of the wish that the slain animal may rise again, in this world or the next one.

animalism. The mysterious relation in hunting cultures between humans and animals manifested, for example, in the idea of spirits in animal form.

annual ceremony of cosmic rejuvenation. The ceremony held each year at the beginning of a new vegetation year to bring humans in harmony with the rejuvenation not only of vegetation and animal life, but also of the world and the cosmos; it is a reiteration of the cosmic drama through which the world was once formed.

apila ashiwanni. Zuni Bow Priests, once war chiefs, associated with the mythical *ahayuta.*

ashiwanni. Zuni Rain Priests.

awonawilona. A class of supernatural beings among the Zuni, in particular the Sun Father and Moon Mother.

bear ceremonialism. The animal ceremonialism centered on the bear; bear ceremonialism is the most developed form of animal ceremonialism.

beast gods. Zuni supernatural masters of animal species.

ceremonial moieties. In some tribes the two halves into which the population is divided for the purpose of alternating at ritual performances; for instance, one moiety is supposed to bury the dead of the other moiety.

circumboreal religion. The religions of the northern woodland

137

areas in North America and Eurasia. They include animal ceremonialism, beliefs in masters of the game, worship of sky gods and atmospheric spirits, and shamanism.

circumpolar religion. The religions of northernmost Arctic and sub-Arctic North America and Eurasia which, due to historical and ecological factors, show a certain likeness to each other.

couvade. The custom of the husband undergoing certain taboos and ritual injunctions during the latter part of his wife's pregnancy.

Coyote. The prairie wolf, mythic culture hero and trickster among the Shoshoni.

culture hero. A supernatural being from the beginning of time who introduced cultural and religious institutions among humankind.

dzoavits. Among the Shoshoni, monsters who eat people.

Emanation myth. Myth about the origin of the world in which the world is said to emanate from the sexual union of two divine beings.

Emergence myth. Myth about the emergence of the primeval mankind from the underworld.

ettowe. The mighty fetishes of Zuni Rain Priests.

fetish. Object radiating supernatural power.

Ghost Dance. A revivalistic movement originating among the Paiute of Nevada and California 1870–1890 and spreading to the Plains Indians where it caused clashes between Sioux Indians and the U.S. military. The dance is named for its round-dancing, which was supposed to contribute to the return of the dead and the good times of yore.

intrusion. See spirit or object intrusion.

itiwana. "The middle place," the Zuni center.

kachina. Among the Pueblo Indians a masked dancer and the spirit portrayed by this dancer—usually an ancestor and rain spirit.

kachina priests. The supernatural rulers of the mysterious Kachina Village among the Zuni.

kiva. The Hopi word for a partially subterranean cult chamber among the Pueblo Indians.

koko. The Zuni term for *kachina.*

koyemshi. The *kachina* clowns.

Long Horn. Supernatural master of the deer among the Zuni.

master of the animals. The idea that every animal species of importance has its own supernatural ruler or master who protects the animals of that species and either offers them to or withholds them from the hunters.

medicine. A term usually applied to supernatural power, in particular the power received by an Indian from his or her personal protective spirit.

medicine bag, medicine bundle. A bag or sack of animal skin in which an Indian, a clan or a society keeps its sacred "medicines," that is, pieces of animal bones, claws, hooves, pollen meal, or feathers which constitute centers of sacred power. The bag or bundle is composed according to instructions by guardian spirits in dreams or visions. Some clan or tribal bundles are inherited from one generation to the next and so on. The contents of Zuni bundles are often described as fetishes.

medicine man, medicine woman. A person who has received supernatural power of importance, in particular medical power.

medicine society. A society composed of people blessed by the same supernatural power, in particular curative power.

medicine wheel. Arrangements of stones in circles around a central hub by which certain calendar dates, such as the summer solstice, have been decided.

Mythic Twins. The creative brothers or culture heroes (cf. *ahayuta*); one of them is often identical with the Supreme Being, the other with the trickster.

nagualism. A Mexican Indian term denoting such an intimate connection between an individual and the individual's guardian spirit that they share the same qualities and even the same life.

navushieip. The Shoshoni word for dream or vision and the soul that has such experiences (the "dream soul").

nyipij. "Wind master," the Shoshoni spirit controlling the winds.

nynymbi. Dangerous dwarf spirits among the Shoshoni.

pandzoavits. See *dzoavits.*

Pan-Indianism. The (American Indian) interpretation that Indian religious symbols basically cover the same concepts in all tribes since all Indians are really ethnically and culturally identical, and the movement to realize this idea.

Pautiwa. The chief of the *kachina* priests in Zuni religion.

Payatamu. Zuni culture hero who introduced corn agriculture.

pekwin. The Sun Priest and spiritual leader of the Zuni.

Peyotism. A revivalistic religion based on the use of peyote, a small spineless psychotropic cactus from the Rio Grande area, that has spread from the southern Plains over the United States and southern Canada.

Poshayanki. Zuni culture hero, head of the beast gods and patron of the medicine societies.

puberty quest. A vision quest at puberty.

pueblo. The Spanish word for "town"; it also means the people of the town. The concentrated Indian adobe settlements of New Mexico and Arizona are called pueblos and the Indians living there Pueblo Indians.

puha. The Shoshoni word both for supernatural power and the guardian spirit that grants such power.

puhagan. In Shoshoni "possessor of supernatural power," the term for a medicine man or woman and any person with such power.

reincarnation. Rebirth as a human.

Santo. Spanish for "saint" (used by the Zuni).

Shalako. The great Zuni ritual at the end of the year; the *shalako* are powerful *kachinas*.

shaman. A religio-magical practitioner who, on behalf of society and with the aid of guardian spirit(s), enters into a trance (ecstasy) to establish contact with the powers in the other world.

shamanism. A complex of rituals, tales, and beliefs concentrated around the shaman.

sipapu. In Pueblo religion the place of emergence from the underworld of the first people, symbolized by a sacred hollow in a cult chamber.

soul loss. The idea that a disease is due to the loss of the patient's soul (or one of his or her souls).

spirit or **object intrusion.** The idea that a disease is due to the intrusion into the body of a spirit or an object.

Sun Dance. The annual cosmic rejuvenation ceremony of the Plains Indians.

taboo. Scientific term taken from the South Sea islanders to denote what is forbidden, dangerous, and sacred; a prohibition with a religious or social sanction.

Tam Apo. "Our Father," the Shoshoni name of the Supreme Being.

tam sogobia. "Our Mother Earth," the Shoshoni goddess of the earth.

tipi. The buffalo skin tent of Plains Indians.

tongwoyaget. "Crying clouds," the Shoshoni thunderbird.

totem poles. Heraldic poles among the Indians of the Northwest Coast raised to celebrate an important person's acquisition of a new name (or title), to commemorate a feast or a ceremonial occasion, or to preserve the remains of a dead person. The poles usually portray guardian spirits and the owner or the owner's ancestors.

transmigration. Rebirth as an animal, tree, or inanimate thing.

trickster. A character in the mythologies of many Native American peoples, often identical with the culture hero in his comic aspects.

uwanammi. Zuni spirits of rain and dew.

vision quest. The ritual quest for a guardian spirit performed by males in early youth or (on the Plains) repeatedly on later occasions and by some females. The Indian seeks the spirit in lone places where it may appear to him or her in a vision.

Wakan Tanka. The collective term for supernatural beings of the Lakota (Dakota) Indians; it is often used to denote the Supreme Being—the interpretations of the Indians vacillate between spirit collectivity and a High God.

Wolf. The chief of the Shoshoni myth world, among the Wind River Shoshoni corresponding to the Supreme Being of everyday religion.

World Tree. The Cosmic tree that stretches through three worlds—sky, earth, and underworld; it is a symbol of the cosmic center or the Supreme Being, and serves as a communications channel between the sky powers and humans.

Selected Reading List

Benedict, Ruth. *Zuni Mythology.* 2 vols. Columbia University Contributions to Anthropology 21. New York: Columbia University Press, 1935.

———. *Patterns of Culture.* London: Routledge, 1946.

Bunzel, Ruth L. "Introduction to Zuñi Ceremonialism," "Zuñi Origin Myths," "Zuñi Ritual Poetry," "Zuñi Katcinas." *47th Annual Report of the Bureau of American Ethnology.* Washington, 1932.

Cazeneuve, Jean. *Les dieux dansent à Cibola.* Paris: Gallimard, 1957.

Cushing, Frank H. "Zuñi Fetiches." *2nd Annual Report of the Bureau of Ethnology.* Washington, 1883.

———. "Outlines of Zuñi Creation Myths." *13th Annual Report of the Bureau of Ethnology.* Washington, 1896.

———. *Zuñi: Selected Writings.* Edited by Jesse Green. Lincoln, Nebr.: University of Nebraska Press, 1979.

Handbook of North American Indians, vol. 9, *Southwest,* edited by William C. Sturtevant and Alfonso Ortiz. Articles on the Zuni by, among others, Fred Eggan, Edmund J. Ladd, and Dennis Tedlock. Washington: Smithsonian Institution, 1979.

Hultkrantz, Åke. *Belief and Worship in Native North America.* Edited by Christopher Vecsey. Syracuse, N.Y.: Syracuse University Press, 1981.

Kirk, Ruth F. "Introduction to Zuni Fetishism." *Papers of the School of American Research.* Santa Fe, N. Mex., 1943.

Lowie, Robert H. "The Northern Shoshone." *Anthropological Papers of the American Museum of Natural History,* vol. 2, part 2. New York, 1909.

Parsons, Elsie Clews. "Notes on Zuñi." *Memoirs of the American Anthropological Association* 4, nos. 3–4. Lancaster, Pa., 1917.

———. "Hopi and Zuñi Ceremonialism." *Memoirs of the American Anthropological Association* 39. Menasha, Wis., 1933.

———. *Pueblo Indian Religion.* 2 vols. Chicago: University of Chicago Press, 1939.

Quam, Alvina, ed. *The Zunis: Self-Portrayals.* Albuquerque, N. Mex.: University of New Mexico Press, 1972.

Roediger, Virginia More. *Ceremonial Customs of the Pueblo Indians.* Berkeley and Los Angeles: University of California Press, 1961.

Shimkin, Demitri B. "The Wind River Shoshone Sun Dance." *Bureau of American Ethnology,* Bulletin 151. Washington, 1953.

Stevenson, Matilda Coxe. "The Zuñi Indians: Their Mythology, Esoteric Fraternities, and Ceremonies." 23rd *Annual Report of the Bureau of American Ethnology.* Washington, 1904.

Voget, Fred W. *The Shoshoni-Crow Sun Dance.* Norman, Okla.: University of Oklahoma Press, 1984.